Anonymous

Rameses the Great

Or, Egypt 3300 years ago

Anonymous

Rameses the Great
Or, Egypt 3300 years ago

ISBN/EAN: 9783337323400

Printed in Europe, USA, Canada, Australia, Japan

Cover: Foto ©ninafisch / pixelio.de

More available books at **www.hansebooks.com**

WONDERS OF ART AND ARCHÆOLOGY

RAMESES THE GREAT

OR

EGYPT 3300 YEARS AGO

Translated from the French of F. De Lanoye

ILLUSTRATED

NEW YORK
CHARLES SCRIBNER'S SONS
1885

LIST OF ILLUSTRATIONS.

Rameses Mei-Amoun. From the alabaster statue in the Museum of the Louvre. (*Frontispiece.*)

	PAGE
The Pyramids and the Sphinx	9
Peoples known to the Egyptians	17
The Temple of Denderah (restored)	27
The Smaller Temple at Philæ	39
The Temples of Philæ (restored)	43
Hypostylic Hall at Karnak	55
The Avenue of Rams	71
An Egyptian Princess	75
The Interior Court of Karnak	81
The Sphinx of Rameses II.	87
Royal Scribes	109
Egyptian Cavalry	113
Egyptian Infantry	119
Bas-relief of Sesostris	123
Asiatic Enemies of the Egyptians	131
Rameses in Battle	139
The City of Atesh	147
Pylons and Portico of a Grand Temple	169
View of Thebes during an Inundation	173
Colossi of Amenoph III., or Memmon	177
A Palace Temple of Thebes (bird's-eye view)	181
The Residence of an Egyptian of rank	185
The Rameseum. Hall of the Colossus	189
The Rameseum. Hall of the Caryatides	193

LIST OF ILLUSTRATIONS.

Slaves under the Eighteenth Dynasty, making brick	197
Captives building a Temple	201
A Hypostylic Hall	203
Present Aspect of Ibrim	217
The Speos of Athor	221
The Speos of Phra	225
Interior of the Speos of Phra	229
Façade of the Speos of Ipsamboul	233
A Mummy in its Bandages	238
Case containing a Mummy	239
Interior Coffin	239
Exterior Coffin	240
Sarcophagus	241
Royal Cartouche of Rameses Mei-Amoun	245
Hieroglyphics of the Names of Egyptian Kings	251, 257
Asiatic Nomads	281

CONTENTS.

THE CAMPAIGNS OF RAMESES THE GREAT.

PAGE

The Basin of the Nile and its First Colonists.—Races of Men known in Egypt Fifteen Centuries before the Birth of Christ.—Pre-Historic Chronology of the Egyptian Empire.—Menes, the First Founder of a Dynasty.—Discordance between Epigraphy and Geology.—The Irruption of the Hycsos.—National Rivalries and Wars.—The Eighteenth Dynasty.. 1

RAMESES II.

Rameses II.—Mei-Amoun the Great, otherwise known as Sesostris.—The Names of Rameses; his Childhood; his Youth; his Coronation.—A Consecration Thirty-three Centuries Ago.—Social Rank in Egypt, and the People, at that Period of its History........................... 61

THE CAMPAIGNS OF RAMESES THE GREAT.

Situation, Wealth and Population of Egypt, on the Accession of Rameses.—The plausible Motives for his Expeditions.—Two Razzias at an Interval of Thirty-three Centuries.—Departure of Rameses for Asia.—His Army.—Testimony of Tacitus, Herodotus, Strabo and the Monuments.—A Bulle-

CONTENTS.

tin of Victory, and a Poet Laureate of the Fourteenth Century before our Era.—The Battle of Atesh.—The return of Rameses.. 97

THE MONUMENTS OF RAMESES THE GREAT.

The Testimony of Herodotus, of Diodorus, and of the Bible.—Memphis and Thebes.—the Great Days of Royalty.—An Artesian Well in the time of Rameses.—The Land of Cush. — The Spears of Ipsamboul.—The old Age of Rameses.—Skeletons of Oxen and Skeletons of Kings.—Darius and the Statue of Rameses............................ 161

APPENDIX.

I. The Cushites................................. 249
II. The Temple of Denderah...................... 250
III. The Ancient Bed of the Nile.................. 252
IV. The Shepherd King Apapias and the God Sutekh..... 253
V. The Names of Rameses II..................... 254
VI. The Images of Ancestors..................... 257
VII. The Army of Rameses II.—the Military Caste........ 261
VIII. The Robus................................ 263
IX. Manners and Customs of the Egyptians............. 264
X. The Stele of the Temple of Khons................ 281
XI. Chronological Canon, or Table of the Dynasties and Kings of Egypt.................................. 287

EGYPT BEFORE THE TIME OF RAMESES.

The Basin of the Nile and its First Colonists.—Races of Men known in Egypt Fifteen Centuries before the Birth of Christ.—Pre-Historic Chronology of the Egyptian Empire.—Menes, the First Founder of a Dynasty.—Discordance between Epigraphy and Geology.—The Irruption of the Hycsos.—National Rivalries and Wars.—The Eighteenth Dynasty.

I.

When the traveller from Europe directs his course toward the southeast angle of the Mediterranean, he must not expect to see the African country reveal itself to his gaze in those majestic aspects to which the Alpine landscapes of Liguria, the Tyrrhenian Islands, Italy or Greece may have accustomed him. Upon that part of the African coast which directly confronts Asia Minor, there is nothing of the kind; a reddish mist, due, no doubt, to the rarefaction of the atmosphere, heated by the combined action of the sand and the sun, is the first indication of the vicinity of land that appears on the horizon: the second is presented by the sight of a few palm-tree tops reflected high in the air by the refraction of the vapory mass. At length, almost at the moment when you are about to touch it, the low, sandy beach that sustains them is seen, like a thin, reddish line, a feeble boundary between the deep green of the sea and the pale blue of the heavens.

Beyond that line, marshes whose extent has earned them the title of lakes, and moving sands, are forever renewing with the fertility of the soil, and the cultivation bestowed upon it, the antique struggle between the two brothers Typhon and Asiri.* Then, behind that second zone, a wide plain, almost level with the water and intersected by numerous canals, extends toward the south, gradually narrowing as it goes, up to the point where these canals and the river which feeds them diverge in a triangle toward the sea. This river is the Nile: this plain is its Delta, a tract periodically submerged for three months at a time, by the waters that have formed it,—" a carpeting of verdure, of flowers and

---

* This we think is the more exact spelling of the classic *Osiris*. Asiri = Asura, one of the oldest titles employed by man to designate God. See E. Burnouf's Commentary on the Yaena: and Jean Reynaud's study on Zoroaster.

of rich harvests from November until March,—a cracked and burning soil, laden with a black, impalpable dust during the remainder of the year,"—says Amrou in a letter to the Caliph Omar.

At the apex of the Delta, the horizon ascends and gradually contracts from the southeast toward the west. At that point, the crests of the hills which, all the way from the ridges of Upper Africa, shut in the narrow valley of the Nile between their parallel chains and shelter it from the continually threatening invasions of the deserts that it crosses, subside and are at length lost beneath the sand. At the foot of the Mokattan, the last broad slope of the Arabian chain, stretches the modern city of Cairo. Nearly opposite, on the left bank of the river, a salient angle of the Libyan chain serves as a pedestal to the eternal pyramids whose gigantic shadows the setting sun flings far over the groves of palm trees that now cover the space where Memphis stood.

"Placed at the entrance of the valley of the Nile," says Chateaubriand in *Les Martyrs*, "they look like the mourning portals of Egypt, or rather like some triumphal monument reared to Death to commemorate his victories. Pharaoh is there with all his people, and their sepulchres are around him!"

II.

Six degrees of latitude separate this point from the one where almost immediately under the tropic circle, the Nile, traversing the granitic rocks of Syene and of Philæ, penetrates the Egyptian territory. Beyond, toward the South, extends Nubia. In this space of more than four hundred and fifty miles in length, by a breadth of nearly twenty, the brilliant glow of the sky, the freshness of the waters, the fertility of the plain and the aridity of its borders; the extreme pettiness of all the traces that modern man has left of his presence, and the colossal seal of the antique generations,—contrasts of every kind, in a word,—seem to be accumulated, to strike the beholder with prolonged astonishment.

Here the geologist may recognize, as he does in the Delta, a conquest won by the dry land over the sea,—a gulf filled up, since the last great astronomical revolution of our globe, by deposits of clay that the lapse of ages had heaped there after it had been washed down, each spring, from the abrupt slopes of Abyssinia and from those other mountains, unknown until yesterday, but suspected, for two thousand years, to be in existence, which, away beyond the Equator, conceal the long-sought-for sources of the Nile.

Here, too, the antiquary and the poet may contemplate the most gigantic efforts of plastic art that any race has left behind it: temples, palaces, tombs, obelisks and colossal figures half ruined and buried beneath the sand; crypts cut out in the solid rock; catacombs; cities of the dead perpetuating in the very entrails of the desert mountains, those ruins which were the cities of the living!—a long avenue of fragments and remains dating back to an epoch whereof history lacked the annals more than twenty centuries ago, but which the correlation of the monuments, the religious notions and the institutions of an entire people with the surroundings in the midst of which it grew, seem to characterize so peculiarly that no other epoch could comprehend or explain its fundamental meaning and creative idea, much less successfully attempt to take them for a model.

III.

It was reserved for the generation that is dying out to penetrate, and not in vain, the depths of these enigmatical ruins; to disentomb from them the past, and to restore to it the real aspect that once it wore, along with a part of its lost chronology.

Thanks to the acquisitions of modern science, for whose progress the genius and the blood of France have helped to clear the way; thanks to the unhoped-for deciphering of those monumental inscriptions through which the Egyptians of forty centuries ago seem still to converse with the men of our own time, the historian can at length present to them upon their sepulchres testimony more certain and reliable than classic antiquity, in the days of its decline, could offer in their behalf.

Although the idea of again securing the thread, a hundred times broken, of Egyptian tradition, must be once for all abandoned, we have it in our power to reconstruct the most brilliant part of it almost to perfection. The period that it covers flourished in times which nations the most jealous of their antiquity do not, in their authentic records, pretend to have attained.

Henceforth, enabled to appreciate the weight of Egypt in the balance of the world, historical criticism is called upon, also, to judge of the manner in which she has fulfilled the functions that seemed to have been assigned to her by Providence, viz., the protection of nascent civilization against the native barbarism of the wandering tribes that hung around

The Pyramids and The Sphinx.

its outskirts, and the initiation of the savage races of the Mediterranean valley into the peaceful mysteries of agriculture and industry. In fine, it is easy to make out how the empire must have perished, and its colossal model have disappeared from the Earth, on the day when humanity ceased to be split up into a few hostile groups, separated as much by space as by animosity; and when the vital energy of social communities, the exclusive privilege, at first, of castes and classes restricted in number, began to be distributed among all the members of the social body.

IV.

The lofty plateau of equatorial Africa that extends beyond the fifteenth degree of north latitude in Abyssinia and the twelfth in the Wadai, seems to recede, between those two extreme points, as far southward as some distance beyond the Equator, whence it sinks towards the North, in a vast concave depression, of which the Nile occupies the lowest part.

Issuing from the only source worthy of it, a sort of fresh water sea covering the highest levels of this table-land, the great African river that, to use the expression of Herodotus, *has created Egypt*, descends by a series of cataracts into the plains of the Baris, the Djirs and the Donkas, which are dotted with lakes and streamlets, and then into the country where the Shillooks have taken the place of the old *Automoli* or refugees.* The water sheds on its left, pour into its tide during this journey a great number of tributaries which are still unnamed in history. On the other hand, the Abyssinian mountain mass sends to it, on its right bank, some powerful affluents of which two at least, the Abawi and the Taccaze were known to the earliest geographers under the names Astapus and Astaboras

A characteristic trait of this river, and one that at first sight distinguishes it on the map of the globe, is the rectilinear direction of its basin. The 30th meridian eastward of Paris, one of the three that traverse the great sheet of water know as Lake Nyanza, crosses one of the mouths of the Delta at the distance of a thousand leagues from there, and during the interval the Nile, that seems to entwine

---

* Herodotus gives this name to the Egyptians who abandoned their country, under the reign of Psammeticus, in consequence of the intrusion of foreigners into public office, and of Greek and Ionian *condottieri* into the ranks of the army.

itself around it like the sacred *uræus* around the antique *caduceus*, intersects it eight times at least with its windings, without, in any instance, receding more than forty leagues from it in its farthest divergence.

But in other respects, it alone among the great rivers of the world is not swollen by any affluent in the last third of its course, which it pursues in solitary grandeur for the distance of four hundred leagues, between two deserts whose sands, cut off from the rains of the tropics, greedily absorb its waters without yielding it, in return, the tribute of the feeblest rivulet or torrent.

The isolation of this portion of the basin in which it dwelt constituted the strong point of Egyptian society during the period of its development. With few exceptions the migrations of tribes and races that then wandered to the four quarters of the earth, swept past, either above or below it. Herein lay the secret of the form that it assumed; of the prolonged existence that was accorded it, and, let us hasten to add, of its weakness when the hour of its downfall had arrived.

V.

All who have devoted any time to observation of the territory and history of Egypt, from Herodotus to Champollion, were under the impression that the Nile, as it has brought soil and fertility to Egypt, had likewise brought it men and civilization, and that the latter descended with it from the south to the north.

A contrary opinion prevails, at present, among the learned in Egyptian matters. Many of them, those especially who are somewhat under the influence of German philosophy, affirm that the earliest settlers and earliest civilization commenced their work in the basin of the Nile, on the north, and that they ascended, instead of descending, the river.

This difference of opinion is more apparent than real, since it has reference, fundamentally, only to the line followed by the migrations between the point of departure and the point of arrival, and in both hypotheses, the primitive cradle of the Egyptians and of their instructors must be sought for in Asia.

Among the mummies which the Egyptian catacombs and places of burial daily yield to our examination, modern anatomists think that they are able to distinguish three separate classes: the first comprising the ancestors of the Copts properly so-styled, the form of whose crania recalls the shape of the heads of the statuary and the sphinxes of Thebes; the second bears some analogy to the Hindoo type, and the third seems to be akin to the Nubian tribes, and the same savants connect it, as well as the Copts, with the Berber race.

All who still cherish a disciple's remembrance of the eminent men who were the preceptors, so to speak, of those who to-day are the masters of historical science,—of the Volneys, the Heerens and the Ecksteins—will, very justly, be astonished when they miss from among the tribes set down as the ancestors of the ancient Egyptians, the Cushites or Negroes who have left their indelible stamp upon the religious notions of the people. For our part, since we have but little faith in the expression *human races*, but a great deal in the modifications of *the family of man* effected by the combined action of physical and moral surroundings; by the influence of climate; of the rules of health observed, and the institutions maintained, and by the emanations of soil and sun, we shall confine ourselves to another source of information. We shall, upon this much debated subject, question the tombs of the Pharaohs excavated in the Libyan chain to the westward of Thebes, during the lifetime of the princes whose last resting-places they became.

The perfection of the adornment and the finish of the workmanship on each of them are in proportion to the duration of the reign of the guest whom they were to receive. But upon the walls of all of them where time had admitted the finishing stroke, dating from the nineteenth dynasty,* the mysterious artist has carved and painted the images of the principal fractions of the human race known in his time.

Conducted, one and all, by Horus, the pastoral god of the nations, they are generally arranged in four groups corresponding with the four divisions of the world then known. The group farthest away from the god consists of savages of lofty stature, with light or sandy hair, blue eyes, and straight or slightly rounded features. Tattooed and covered with the spoils of the *aurochs* and the bear, just as those late comers in old Europe, the Gauls and the Cimbri, appeared to the affrighted Greeks and Romans, in after ages, did the ancient Pelasgi appear fifteen centuries before the Christian Era, to the erudite and culti-

---

* The nineteenth only. The geographical knowledge which these paintings pre-suppose does not appear to have existed any earlier. This is a good point to establish.

Nubian. Negro. Assyrian. Pelasgian. Arab or Hebrew.
Peoples known to the Egyptians.

vated Egyptians. The latter called them *Tamhus*. In the group that precedes them, are strikingly observable all the characteristics of the negro type in its most degraded varieties, and to these legend gives the name of *Nahazis*.

In advance of them, again, are the representatives of Asia. Their yellow and tawny complexions; their aquiline or beaked noses; their black beards, sharp and pointed on some, ample and curly on others; their costumes of varied hue and fashion, indicate members of the Aramæan branches: Arabs, Hebrews and Assyrians. On some walls, Medes and Ionians figure among these sons of Shem. All of them are comprised in the general denomination of *Aamus*. Lastly, standing close to the heathen divinity, and, as it were, under his special protection, are men of dark red skins and tall slender figure, with gentle and regular countenances, clear cut eyes, straight noses and open facial angle, wearing their hair in plaits, and dressed in white garments. The name of *Rut-n-Rom*—the germ, or the race of man—with which they are specially honored, sufficiently point out the dwellers on the banks of the sacred river,—in other words, the Egyptians.

The typical characteristics here associated with them, identical on all the monuments and verified upon thousands of mummies of different epochs, are not found among the Copts, their mongrel descendants. Amid the confused mixture of all the nations that have succeeded each other in Egypt, the Copts have retained the idiom, better than the blood, of the old race.*

The latter, whose presence may be traced at numerous points on the African continent, is met with again, in all its original purity, in two nations who dwell in the basin of the Nile, but at a wide distance from each other,—the Abyssinians of the upper plains, and the Barabras of lower Nubia, sheltered as they have been, the latter by poverty, the former by the natural strength of their soil, from the invasions of conquerors, and from the current of the migrations which, in the lapse of ages, has passed between them and isolated them, leaving them divided and far apart, yet kindred boughs of a parent trunk that has ceased to exist.

---

* Champollion's Letters on Egypt and Nubia. Larrey's Memoirs, in the Description of Egypt. Caillaud's Journey to Meroe and the White Nile. Trémeaux's Journey to Nubia, etc.

VI.

SHOULD the logic of induction lead us, more than once, in the course of this recital, to admit extracts from Manetho among the material upon which historical conclusions are based, it must not, for that reason, be inferred that we are inclined to accord to the remaining works of that old annalist, and especially to his lists of kings and dynasties, analogous authority.

It is not for us to inquire whether that Egyptian priest, entrusted with the task of collecting in the Greek language all the national traditions stored away among the sacerdotal archives of his country, was or was not equal to his mission. Of the three volumes that composed his work, a few fragments, drowned in the compilations of later periods, and lists of kings revised, corrected and abridged by the monastic zeal of the early Christians, being all, unfortunately, that have come down to us, it would be unjust to hold the author responsible for all the contradictions of dates, facts and figures as well as the double applications that these different fragments contain.

But, when we consider the complete discordance that exists between these documents of common origin and those whence Herodotus had drawn his facts two centuries earlier, and weigh the conflicting views whereby they have strayed from the ancient source that should have supplied them, and which, surviving in our day under the name of the *Old Chronicles*, gives only four hundred and forty-three years to the fifteen earliest dynasties to which Manetho assigns forty or fifty centuries, we must agree with one of the most judicious investigations of antiquity, that it is improbable that an Egyptian priest compiling with all the prejudices of his caste in a foreign tongue, and in behalf of a king whom he regarded as of barbarian origin, the traditions of an expiring nationality scattered on monuments of diverse and often rival purport, should be specially endowed with *that spirit of criticism* in whose default history relapses into legend, and which was almost entirely wanting in the ancients.*

At the close of this work will be found a faithful synopsis of Manetho's lists, such as they emanated from the hands of Julius Africanus, Eusebius and Syncellus: such, too, as Champollion and his successors thought they could make them by correcting the figures according to the monumental inscriptions. We have also reserved the right to range together a certain number of facts, the synchronism

---

* Volney's Researches in ancient History.

of which is well-nigh certain, and may serve to establish some rallying points upon the floating canvas of Egyptian chronology, and prepare for it a framework beyond which it cannot very easily escape.

VII.

It is not consistent with the plan of our book to extend this chronological study any farther. Such as it is, it must suffice the reader for a basis whereon to form his own opinion of the matter, and to choose between the system that would push back into the night of ages the development of the Egyptian nationality, and the one that, relying upon the study of social facts, and upon the nature of man, holds that the more the torch of history gains in clearness, the more concise should chronology become and ancient times approach our own.

The eternal aspiration of the human mind toward a felicity which the present denies it, and which it could not ask of the future, so long as it was unaware of its own progressive faculties, was undoubtedly the source of the mania that impelled all communities to antedate their origin and throw it back into a past that was all the more regretted that its depths were the more obscure. In those days, nations, as in more recent times families, gauged their nobility not by deeds but by the duration of their existence. Hence, for historians jealous as to the origin of their country, arose the necessity of multiplying generations and centuries, and of ranging in series, one after the other, successions of dynasties and parallel epochs, along with contemporaneous men and facts. Hence, too, for Manetho, in particular, the necessity of conforming his annals to the fables credited by the puerile vanity of the priestly order, and of spreading out the real traditions of his country in a chaos without proportion, name or limit.

Serious history, then, cannot carry these traditions farther back than the period where they cease to be controlled by positive synchronic data. The first point of all is the appearance of Argus upon the stage of the world. From astronomical data calculated first by Bailly and Colebrooke, afterwards adopted by Lahsen and Wilson, and finally put beyond all doubt by Laplace, this event, which has furnished roots to the genealogical tree of ancient Egypt, may go back thirty centuries before our era, but no farther.

This opinion, we know, will be taxed as heretical and even blasphemous by those who approach the realm of history not in order to extract therefrom fruitful lessons and hopes for the future, but that they may, in the presence of dusty remains and extravagant legends, give themselves up to the ecstatic admiration of an old idolatry as aimless as it was artificial and out of date. To have Memphis built by Menes, 5800 years before our era, upon the filled-up bed of the Nile diverted from its course; to believe piously in the books of anatomy written by Athoth, the son and successor of the first-named dynastic founder; to unreservedly admit the authenticity of the ancestral images carried before the kings at religious ceremonies,* and the filiation of the three hundred and forty-five *Pi-Romis*† mentioned by Herodotus; to rear the Pyramids of Gizeh in the time of the brothers Supphi

---

* At Rome, also, in many public and private ceremonies, there were exhibited along with the images of ancestors those of the gods to which the Roman patricians pretended to trace their origin. But have modern historians ever come to the conclusion, from the presence of the images of Mars and Venus at the funeral rites of Julius or Martius, that those fetiches of the primitive clans of Latium ever had a real personal existence? Assuredly not. Yet this is what Egyptian investigators do in our day, in regard to Menes and many mythical personages of ancient Egypt.

† This word is equivalent to "the man superior to all others;" "a brave and virtuous person;" "an excellent man." Herodotus. Euterpe, ch. 143.

or Chuffu, of the fourth dynasty, forty or fifty centuries before Christ; and to put back the origin of the grand hydraulic and architectural monuments of Fayoum fifteen hundred years anterior to Thothmes III, to Seti I, to Rameses Mei-Amoun; to cause the conquest of Asia, two thousand five hundred years before the Saviour, by an Osymandyas and a Sesortasen, personages of whom the heroes of the eighteenth and nineteenth dynasties would be merely feeble imitators,—all this was, for a long time in France, and is still in Germany, a source of pleasure even to grave adepts in science, that it would be perilous to disturb by calm discussion. Therefore, we shall not attempt the task, confident as we are, that, ere long, there will become of those mythical legends, what recently became of the series of centuries that our fathers so generously accorded to the temples of Esneh and Denderah—centuries which we had to reduce from sixty-four and from thirty-eight to seventeen or eighteen at the utmost.*

---

* We know that this pretended antiquity was the basis given by Dupuy to his system in his " Origin of Religious Worship." See Appendix II.

The Temple of Denderah (restored according to the Egyptian Commission).

VIII.

Nevertheless, we cannot close this dissertation, which has been too far prolonged, already, for the plan of our book, without reminding those who "do not see what delight there is in shutting themselves up for four thousand years with nations in their infancy and tyrants in decay"* the avowal wrung by Herodotus from the very priesthood of Memphis: "That in the time of Menes, the first *mortal King of Egypt, the entire country below the Thebaic nome was nothing but a marsh.*" But, in regard to the philological identity of the name Menes with that of Manu, given in the Sanscrit tongue, to the spirits proceeding out of Brahma and especially entrusted by him with the charge of giving laws to the Earth, this avowal leaves nothing to the name in question and to the legends therewith connected but the consistency of a myth symbolizing the energetic force of nature in the earliest times, the same being subsequently imported from the banks of the Indus to those of the Nile, at an unknown period by a method of transmission identical with that which has borne the name of Jemshid (Yima

---

* Chateaubriand. Introduction to his Journey to America.

Tchaeto), step by step, from the valleys of the Jaxartes and the Tarim, to the high plains of Media and Persia. In fine, we must ascertain for our readers the result of the researches that modern geology has been making with regard to the beds of clay successively deposited by the periodical inundations of the Egyptian river, and according to which we must not date farther back than some thirty centuries before Christ the appearance of the first human monuments on the primitive soil of Thebes.*

When a trench is dug or any excavation made in the valley of the Nile, there is, *invariably*, found a layer of vegetable earth from 20 to 24 feet in depth, the result of the river's annual deposit. This layer rests directly upon a bed of sea sand. Very minute calculations led the engineers of the great French expedition to Egypt to estimate at 126 *millimètres*, or about .4134 of a foot, per century, the elevation of this alluvial soil. At a later date, Mr. Lebas, the engineer upon whom devolved the task of conveying the obelisk of Luxor to Paris, and the English savant Wilkinson, came to conclusions almost identical, on the same subject, by methods of research different in character but equally exact in detail. Eight metres, 26¼ feet, the greatest thickness, divided

---

* Description of Egypt. Girard's *Mémoire* on Drainage.

by 126 millimetres, or .4134 of a foot, gives us no more than 6350 years of days equal in length to those of our time. Egyptian history, as Manetho and the epigraphists understand it, is not restrained within these narrow limits. What, then, are we to do, unless we bring down to a date much later than Menes and the kings who built the Pyramids, the period when the Egyptians neither employed nor knew any years of longer term than four months. "The proof of this," admits one of the most ardent champions of the high antiquity of Egypt, "is that, later, when the year consisted of twelve months, three seasons were designated, each comprising four months, which were indicated hieroglyphically by the word *ter*, and by a sign *that may mean a season or a year, indifferently.*"*

The lower course of the old Egyptian Nile is, therefore, geologically speaking, one of the most recently formed of the ancient continent, and, if geology be not a vain word, three thousand, aye, four thousand years anterior to Rameses,—five thousand years at most, if the heaping up of the lower deposits are to be, likewise, taken into account,—the soil of Egypt was still oscillating between the billows of the sea, and the rays of the sun. †

---

* Dr. H. de Brugsch, History of Egypt from the earliest period of its existence (Leipzig, 1859, p. 26.)

† See Appendix III.

Hence, the city of This or Thinis, from which the chief of the first Egyptian dynasty was said to have come, was not founded until long afterward.

IX.

NINE or ten centuries later, that is to say after a longer lapse of time than was allotted to any nation of classic antiquity for its birth, development and death, the population of the valley of the Nile is dimly seen attempting a form of civilization of which historians make known to us only the decline.

Subdivided into several groups whereof Beheni in Nubia, Thebes, Heracleopolis, and Memphis, sometimes independent, sometimes tributary cities, but always rivals of each other, were the chief centres, the different populations referred to had for a common bond:

I. Their social organization, founded on the system of castes, the result of successive immigrations and conquests.

II. Their religous creed, arising like their castes from the superposition of different races upon the same soil; a synthetic derivation from the monstrous superstitions of the Cushites, of Semitic Sabaism and Aryan naturalism, it presented, in the individual manifestations of divine power, traces of its triple origin; but, multiplying those manifestations according to the place and the interest of the moment, and upon each rung of the ladder that connects the phenomena of Earth with the invisible world, it could but terminate for the multitude in the grossest fetichism, and, for thinking men, athwart the mystery of the initiations, in those mystical metaphysics of which the Alexandrian school has transmitted only vague echoes to us.

III. Their language, issuing from the same commingled sources, and retaining traces of its origin, yet differing importantly from nome to nome, from metroplis to metropolis, and particularly, from the Thebais to the Delta, but for which, however, the priests had, in the long run, discovered in the numberless array of their fetiches, animate or inanimate, tangible symbols, a graphic representation and a consecrated alphabet whereof every temple had the key.

IV. A method of burial singular, but imperatively required by a long and cruel experience of the periodical inundations of the river, and of the poisonous effluviæ arising from the contact of the waters with the organic remains hidden beneath the soil.

V. Their sedentary life; industrial and agricultural habits, derived, perforce, like social manners and customs, from the imperious exigencies of their dwelling place and the odd shape of its narrow and elongated territorial surface; at the same time, too, from their jealous attachment to the soil, their hatred and contempt for the stranger, and especially, for the wandering tribes of the frontiers, an impure race whose insolent rapacity and greedy herds defiled the earth and impaired its fertility.

What was there wanting to tribes who inhabited the banks of the Nile, at this period of their existence, to form a nation?—One of those catastrophes which bring communities closer together and combine them, as they do individuals—a partnership of perils, struggles, sufferings, reverses and triumphs gone through, side by side.

Providence brought this about

X.

In due time, came rushing headlong across Western Asia, the first migration of nations whereof history has retained the remembrance. Swollen by all the nomadic tribes that it had gathered to it on the way, it fell suddenly upon the valley of the Nile.

Whence came this human avalanche? Josephus seems to indicate Chaldea; Volney speaks of Yemen. Judging by the force of its impetus and the length of time it took for the disappearance of its straggling remnants, by the name accursed that it left in the memory of Egypt, and above all, by the avenging hate that, in later times, repeatedly impelled the Egyptian armies beyond the river Tigris and the Armenian Taurus, we think that it is in Central Asia, the ever-seething cauldron and workshop whence the commissioned races and the scourges of Divine wrath emanate, that we must look for the starting point of the Hycsos.

Written history contains but a few words to sustain our opinion, yet they are formal and characteristic. "Before there were any Medes and Assyrians," says Justinus, in Book II., chapter iii., the Scythians, i. e., a wandering race coming from the north, invaded Asia and held it in subjection for fifteen hundred years."

The prophets of Thebes and of Memphis might have exclaimed, as those of Judea had occasion to do in later years, in the presence of an irruption of similar hordes.

"Behold a people cometh from the north; a mighty nation hath arisen from the loins of the Earth! They carry the bow and the buckler: they break and destroy without pity!—The noise of their coming is like the roaring of the sea.

"They come up as a cloud; their chariots fly as the whirlwind. Woe unto us!

"I looked upon the Earth and it was a desert; I beheld the mountains, and lo they trembled, and all the hills, and they dashed together. I beheld and lo! there was no man, and all the birds of the heavens were fled; * * * all the cities were broken down. * * * The whole land shall be desolate.* * *

"It is a mighty nation, an ancient nation, a nation whose language thou knowest not, neither understandest what they say. * * * Their quiver is an open sepulchre. * * * And they shall eat up thine harvest and thy bread which thy sons and thy daughters should eat."

---

* Jeremiah, ch. iv. v. and viii.

XI.

HERE, the avowal of Manetho should be received with credence; since sapping the foundation of his system of national antiquity, better than any other argument, it must have sorely wounded his pride.

"In the ancient times," he says, "during the reign of one of our kings named Timaos, the anger of God was aroused against us, I know not why; and there came from the direction of the east a multitude of men of ignoble race who, precipitating themselves by surprise upon our country, possessed themselves of it *without a struggle and with the greatest ease*. They slew part of the chiefs and cast the rest into chains. They burnt our cities and threw down the temples of the gods. Their barbarity toward the Egyptians were such that all who had not perished by the sword were reduced with their women and children to the hardest servitude.

"They then took one from among themselves named Salatis, for a king, and he made his seat at Memphis and subjected all the provinces, superior and inferior alike, to tribute, by occupying them with military garrisons.

"The latter he established principally in the direction of the east, with a view to closing the gates of his conquest against the future masters of Asia.

Having discovered in the Saitic nome or district to the eastward of the Bubastic branch of the Nile, a convenient spot called Avaris (Wara), he fortified it, and placed within its confines and in its neighborhood, two hundred and forty thousand warriors.

Every year, at harvest time, he quited Memphis to come to that place, to superintend the harvests, to pay the salaries and wages, to exercise the multitude in warlike evolutions, and thus inspire the vanquished and foreigners with a salutary fear. Dying after a reign of nineteen years, he had for a successor Beon, who was replaced by Apachnas, to whom succeeded Apophis, then Janas, then Assis, in all, six kings in 259 years and three months." During this whole space of time, they never ceased to wage a war of extermination on the Egyptian race, and they were called the *Hycsos* or Shepherd Kings, for *hac* in the sacred tongue means *king*, and *sos* in the vulgar idiom a shepherd.*

A curious document which has come down to us from those remote times yields the support of irrefutable testimony to Manetho's recital. There may be read on a hieratic papyrus in the British Museum the following inscription :

"It happened that the land of Egypt fell into the

---

* Extract of Manetho in Flavius Josephus, *contra Appionem*.

View of Phila. The Smaller Temple.

hands of strangers (Aad-tus) and then there were no native Pharaohs left in the whole country. At that time their descendant, Ra-Sekenen, was nothing but a *hac*, or chief, of Upper Egypt. The Aad-tus held the *strong city of the sun* * and their king, his majesty Apapias, resided at Ha-War.† The whole country was tributary to him, and brought him all its good productions after the example of the lower country (Lower Egypt).

"And his majesty Ra-Apapias chose the god Sutech as his Lord, and would not be the worshipper of any other god in the entire region, and he built a temple to him in good imperishable stone :"‡

In the presence of text so specific and formal as this, what becomes of the forty preceding centuries of administrative and territorial unity? What remains of all that systematic scaffolding?—unless it be the undeniable proof that the Egypt of those days succumbed so easily, only through the absence of unitary institutions and traditions,—the inanity of her past existence as a nation.

---

* This designation may be applied to Thebes, as well as to Heliopolis.

† This word, which is entirely Aryan in origin, would suffice to indicate the primitive country of the Hycsos. *War*, in the Zend language, means the original enclosure built by Jemshid.—*Wara* or *War*, in Pehlvi, or old Persian, meaning *borough*, *fortified enclosure*.

‡ See Appendix IV.

Surprised amid the pre-occupations inherent to the long infancy in which her servile education kept her under the yoke of religious and royal formalism; parcelled out by the rival pretensions of her various tribes, her cities and her two controlling castes; more accustomed to luxurious pageants, to religious chantings and processions sweeping past from temple to temple along her sacred river, than inured to warlike exercises and the din of battle; better skilled in handling the hoe that fertilizes the soil and the chisel that carves decorations in granite for the hours of peace, than in brandishing the bow and shield which would have saved her in the hour of peril, Egypt fell completely prone before the Hycsos and disappeared for a time beneath the billows of invasion.

The latter, sweeping all before it with barbarian fury, frenzied as it was by the fanaticism of an image-breaking creed, halted only at the limits which nature herself had set to its easy conquest. Those limits were the rocky mountain ranges that a little below the Tropic, and parallel to it, extended from the Libyan desert to the shores of the Red Sea.

The Temples of Philæ (restored according to the Egyptian Commission).

XII.

A DEEP ravine with steep declivities; a river in it studded with a labyrinth of small islands and sharp projections of dark granite constantly embrowned by the dash and the foam of the waves, marks the passage of this mountain chain across the Nile, and constitutes the phenomenon of the cataracts of Syene, so strangely exaggerated by classic antiquity. A little higher up than these rapids rises the Island of Philæ where Egyptian mythology placed the tomb of Asiri, and where, in fact, seemed to terminate, with Egypt itself, the furrow of fertility which the river opens from that point to the sea.

Upon both banks of the Nile, enormous masses of brown freestone and granite, of sombre and calcined hue, confused and upturned at their base, rise, like the chosen scene where Nephtis and Typhon, the gods of the desert and of chaos, had triumphed, and shutting in the horizon of the mysterious isle on all sides, contrast, in the most startling manner, with the white pylons and the regular colonnades that cover its surface.

From this point to the Island of Say in Middle Nubia, this heap of rocks stamped with the seal of desolation, ascends the valley of the Nile, and encloses it with its abrupt acclivities, in such manner as to leave it only the aspect of a mountain torrent which at certain points is but a stone's throw across. A steep path painfully winds along its rugged slopes, and below, at their foot, are seen some narrow furrows of barley and *dourah*, with occasional clumps of date trees indicating a thin strip of cultivable land, which, a hundred times intercepted by jutting ridges of rock rarely attains more than 355 feet in breadth, and supports hardly one hundred thousand inhabitants, upon a surface of more than one hundred and fifty leagues in longitudinal extent.

XIII.

YET, this poor country, this *region of stones*, as the Arabs call it, in their energetic idiom,—the *Baln* or *Dar-el-hazhar*,—was the salvation of rich and fertile Egypt, in the days of Hycsos rule. It gave refuge behind its granite frontier to all the vanquished who had been fortunate enough to escape the sword or the yoke of the invaders. It offered them, in the jagged recesses of its rocks, temples for their gods, palaces for their princes, and rallying places for their warriors. All drank in from its rude hospitality the energy that they lacked, and little by little, it changed to thoughts of vengeance and the hope of return, the regrets they had bestowed on their lost country. The very insufficiency of the Nubian soil to support their number, augmented as it was each day by fresh fugitives, strengthened their resolution. In order to subsist, they were forced to venture upon marauding expeditions into the country that they had not been able to defend. They had to creep stealthily toward it, through the wilderness, and, exposed to constant peril, to snatch away by dint of arms, a portion of the fruits and harvests that it lavished on the stranger. This Bedouin existence perforce accustomed the military caste to danger, and they were recruited by all who had a heart or an arm at the service of their destitution or their resentment. Partial successes developed courage and confidence; allies came to the Egyptians, undoubtedly, from the depths of Ethiopia, and, very probably, from the coasts of India; their expeditions, as they multiplied, became more regular in form and assumed a more general character; their warfare, from being clandestine and fitful became open and continual, until, finally, it took permanent foothold in all the passes that descend from the south into Egypt, recovering ground, step by step, from the Hycsos. Holy work! in which many generations were consumed and which was transmitted from father to son, for more than two hundred years.

The chieftains who, by reason of their descent from the ancient kings, or through services rendered to the common cause, were summoned to direct this great struggle, shared all its vicissitudes. At first mere chiefs of bands roving among the rocks and over the deserts, then sovereigns of Nubia and the Thebais, victory and national consent made them, successively, masters of the Heptanomis and of the lower course of the great river. There are many names, now the subject of dispute between authorities skilled in Egyptian lore who refer them back to still earlier times, which we think belong to the period and range that we are just describing. At length, when Ahmes, the founder of the eighteenth dynasty, uniting all the native forces of the Nile valley, entered Memphis in triumph, drove all the strangers beyond the river to their entrenched camp at Wara, and afterwards expelled them even from that; and when Amenoph, his son, completed their explusion from the territory of Kemi by fresh victories on the roads leading to Asia, these princes may have thought of reconstructing only the past, but, in reality, they set up a totally unknown order of things and ideas.

Upon the ruins of the old principalities of Thebes, Memphis and Fayoum, trampled out by the feet of the Hycsos, worn away and jumbled together by two centuries and a half of battles, they laid what was the real foundation of Egyptian nationality, the true groundwork of a new empire whose strong and stable unity was long to remain without a counterpart in the future, as it was without one in the past.

XIV.

Such were, for Egypt, the final consequences of her first struggle with the men of the north. History, which faithfully credits nations with the tears and the blood that similar crises cost them, and which does not always have the opportunity, as it has in this instance, to correctly estimate their prolific results, must record these with eagerness.

It is to this period of general revival, that we must also refer a fact, the date of which the ancients, failing to discover its origin in the historical ages of Egypt, have pushed back into the night of time, so as to do honor to Menes, a veritable sphinx to whom they committed the keeping of all the problems that they deemed impenetrable. We allude to the reform which substituted the warrior for the priestly caste, at the head of the hierarchy, and which withdrew the kings from the shadow of the temples and the tutelage of the clerical order, to centralize all power in them, and to make them, for a long series of generations, the representatives of all the energies of society.

In the system of the old legendary writers this reform can be explained only by some violent revulsion, or by a usurpation of rights revolting against rights acquired. In our opinion, it proceeded from the grand onward sweep of human affairs; it was ordained by the inflexible logic of events. The latter, in creating new duties, naturally displaced the rights of various classes, and, naturally also, bestowed the greatest share of privilege upon those who undertook the greatest share of responsibility. Such were the men who, in the presence of the victorious stranger, covered with their bosoms and their swords the last asylums of their families and their gods, and repurchased a country for them at the price of their blood. Such men were preferred to those who, seeking refuge in the depths of their sanctuaries, had offered nothing to the common cause but sterile appeals and vain speculations on the enigma of the world.

XV.

The vital sap so superabundant in all nations in a state of social renovation, was with the Egyptians when they had become, in their turn, the conquerors of the Hycsos, in proportion to the time and the sacrifices that victory had cost them.

It developed, afterward, for centuries, from generation to generation, revealing itself, on all sides in striking displays;—at home by gigantic achievements of art or of public utility; outside, by incessant effort to expand in the most opposite directions the boundaries of the Empire, until the latter, at length, overflowed upon the world in civilizing colonies and in warlike expeditions which by ideas or by the sword, by trade or conquest, fertilized the soil where other races were to spring up and grow great in their turn.

If we are to believe the testimony deduced from the monuments, most of the sovereigns who, at that time, reigned in Egypt, had to contend not only against the barbarians of the north and of the south; to repel fresh attacks of the Hycsos, who could not make up their minds to abandon forever the grand prize that their fathers had won,—and to hurl them back into the heart of Asia; but they had, also, to restore the majesty of the altar and the throne by re-erecting the temples and palaces destroyed by time and invasion, and to re-open by agriculture and by canals that should distribute the fertilizing properties of the Nile, sources of Egypt's territorial wealth.

"In no country," wrote the last and the greatest of Egypt's conquerors, on this subject, "in no country has the administration so much influence over public prosperity. If the administration be good, the canals are well dug, well kept, the rules for irrigation are properly executed, the flooding is more complete. If the administration be bad, corrupt or weak, the principles of the system by which the country is watered are violated by seditions factions or by the interests of particular persons or localities; the canals are choked with mud: the dykes are poorly kept, and the entire nation suffers. Other governments have no control over the snow or the rain that falls in this province or in that, but in Egypt, it has a direct influence over the extent and character of the Nile inundations, which take the place of the showers and drifts that fall elsewhere." *

Numerous attestations deduced from publi

---

* Napoleon. *Memoirs Dictated at St. Helena:* Campaign in Egypt.

monuments, and even from the tombs of private persons, agree in bearing witness that the sons and grandsons of Ahmes did not fall short of their mission as warriors and administrators.

Among them, three Amenophs and four Thothmes held sway in Nubia and Syria. Thothmes III., the most celebrated of all, extended the frontiers of the empire as far as the borders of the Tigris to the eastern limits of Mesopotamia.

It is to this period of success and development that Egypt owed an acquisition more valuable for her, and more durable, too, than the annexation of territories distant from her natural frontiers. This was the possession of *the horse* and its healthful domestication on the borders of the Nile.* Strange as it may appear in view of the extreme antiquity ascribed to Egyptian civilization, it cannot be denied that *the noblest conquest that man ever made* remained unknown in Egypt until the seventeenth century preceding our era; and this fact alone suffices to annihilate any system of history tending to assign to Egypt any activity beyond the borders of the valley of the Nile earlier than the eighteenth dynasty.

"The lists of the contributions exacted by

---

* Dr. H. Brugsch. History of Egypt p. 25.

Thothmes III.," says the Vicomte de Rougé, in his Memoir on the Campaigns of Sesostris, "at the close of fourteen expeditions directed chiefly against the Assyrians and the Phœnicians, reveal to us Nineveh and Babylon, Asshur and Shinar bringing in their tribute as vassals to Egypt. They are accompanied by other nations more powerful at that time in Asia than they, but whose names have shone less conspicuously in succeeding ages. During time of peace, the Pharaohs exercised their supremacy regularly in those countries. Leaving all authority in the hands of the national chiefs, they contented themselves with levying an annual tribute. They had, nevertheless, seized the best domains of the vanquished princes, and had appropriated the revenues either to the use of different temples, or to heir personal treasury. Fortresses commanded the chief approaches to Asia; governors at the head of strong garrisons watched the conquered provinces; and when a royal reign lasted for some length of time, the king himself was seen coming to Asia, either peaceably to receive tribute, or angrily to chastise rebels by one of those terrible forays which, in the East, seem to be the very essence of war.

"The concluding reigns of the eighteenth dynasty were agitated by usurpations and religious dissen-

Hypostyle Hall of Karnak (the Central Nave restored according to the Egyptian Commission).

sions. Favored by these disorders, Asia shook off the yoke of the Pharaohs, and Seti I., the Sethos of historians, found the revolt pushed on as far as the gates of Lower Egypt, so that he had to begin over again the conquest of Syria. The victories that signalized the first years of his reign appear to have re-established the Egyptian supremacy over the Asiatic provinces, for some length of time.

The grand hypostylic hall of Karnak, and the magnificent tomb discovered by Belzoni, are majestic monuments, that sufficently attest the tranquillity of the country, the wealth of the monarch, and the high perfection of the arts under the reign of Sethos

But the glory of these names and of these deeds is founded, for posterity, upon the still more dazzling splendor of the second period of that grand Egyptian cycle which, until our day, was entirely comprised in the legend of Sesostris, but which is henceforth eclipsed by the reign, the name, the monuments of Rameses the Great.

RAMESES II.

Rameses II.—Mei-Amoun the Great, otherwise known as Sesostris.—The Names of Rameses; his Childhood; his Youth; his Coronation.—A Consecration Thirty-three Centuries Ago.—Social Rank in Egypt, and the People, at that Period of its History.

I.

THE name of the man whose place we are seeking to fix, and whose active part in history we would make plain to our readers recalls the exaltation of human personal position to the highest limits of pride and power, and the most excessive concentration, in one individual, of all the vital forces of a people that historical annals record. Yet, the name and the individual referred to, had remained enveloped in doubt and uncertainty until our day.

In vain have the chisel and the pencil perpetuated both upon the finest monuments in the valley of the Nile. In vain in the basreliefs that adorn the sanctuaries of the temples and the halls of the palaces, whereof the great Rameses was the founder, has the hyperbole of flattery been pushed so far as to cause the likeness of the supreme Egyptian deity, Ammon-Ra, to appear among those of the monarch. Ammon bestows the empire of the world, both sea and land, upon him, "his well-beloved child, the guardian sun of justice, Rameses II." Along with the image of this heathen god, is seen that of Sethos, the god of war, "who promises him a secure and upright life upon the throne of the sun, forever." With these are also found the portraits of Maut (primeval and prolific Night), and of Isis and Anuke, who dandle Ammon on their knees, refresh this singular bantling with their milk, and endow him, by virtue of this divine nourishment, with "a future prolonged for endless periods of panegyrics."* . . . . Strange confusion and extinction of all things here below! through causes of which the present condition of society permits us to get only a glimpse,† the name and personality of Rameses Mei-Amoun became

---

* *Panegyrics* were the grand state occasions when the fame of the princes and the glory of the gods of Egypt were publicly extolled and celebrated with processions, chantings and festivities.

† See Appendix V.

mixed up, gradually, with those of his father and of two of his descendants. Greece, that grand voice which fills the trumpet of fame, knew nothing of him excepting the mythical remembrances that emerged from this confusion, and which Manetho, the only annalist of his native country, could not or would not clear away. The written history of antiquity contains but one exact mention of him, and this it owes to Tacitus; and it has required all the progress of modern science applied to the researches of the past to enable some of our contemporaries to exhume the real name of the Egyptian hero, and the true part that belongs to him in the furrow which the old land has worn through the years of antiquity. This they accomplished at last, when thirty centuries had rolled away, by disputing with the sands of the desert, the monumental legends of Nubia and the Thebais.

Yet, after all, it matters but little to the history of humanity whether Rameses II. was a member of the eighteenth dynasty, as Champollion thought, or with his grandfather Rameses I., his father Seti I., and Menephta and Seti II., his son and grandson, made up the nineteenth dynasty, as some of the successors of the above-named writer hold.— What interests us, at our great distance in time from Rameses, is to form some idea of the political and social condition of the world when he was summoned to agitate it with the sceptre and the sword: and also to comprehend the elements that had prepared the state of things of which he was, as it were, the consequence, and also those the germs of which he left behind him. We have already, in our former book, endeavored to set forth the first; and in the following pages we shall strive to complete our review by extending it to the second.

II.

Son of Seti I. and of the Queen Twea—the second wife of that prince—Rameses Mei-Amoun must have been born during the quarter of a century that preceded the year 1400 before our Era. The long duration attributed to his reign, and the place that Moses held after him in chronoogy, do not admit of the date of this event falling any later. It was, says Diodorus, the occasion of *an act magnificent and truly royal.* The recital that the Greek historian has transmitted to us on this subject is tinged with the marvellous, as his readers may remember, the dream in which a god announces to Pharaoh that the empire of the Earth is promised to the child just born; the means conceived by the happy father to prepare his son for this high destiny; all the young Egyptians born on the same day with the little prince, gratuitously furnished with nurses and teachers, subsequently brought together around him and with him subjected to a complete education and discipline, made common to them all, so that he might, one day, find in the companions and the studies of his childhood, instruments devoted to him and worthy of his designs as a man and his glory as a King. Then, Arabia and Libya conquered; their deserts traversed and their wild beasts subdued, formed, so to speak, the climax of this masculine education, and, as it were, the first essay in the field made by the prince and his young brethren in arms.

If, in the monuments discovered, nothing has been found to confirm the legendary part of this narrative, at the same time nothing has been found to invalidate it. History sees no objection there to her admitting that Seti was the fortunate adversary of the Asiatic nations, and that, in one of his triumphs, he was enabled to display the images and captives taken from forty-eight of them whom he had subdued, the prisoners saluting him and applauding him as *the son of the Sun, the Lord of diadems, the favorite of Phtah, the good Deity, sovereign of two worlds and eternal as the Sun itself!*" That such a man as this should have dreamed still greater things for his son, and that he should have surrounded the boy's education with all sorts of precautions and all the incitements that could favor his designs, when, at that age of humanity, he had power exalted to the height of divine control at his disposal, is not, by any means, incredible.

Still more: the monuments show us Rameses associated with the crown from his earliest infancy, and receiving the homage of the Egyptians while in his cradle. " You were yet in the egg," his subjects say to him, " and you had the honors of a prince. *While still a very little child, wearing plaited hair, no monument was made without you. . . . . At the age of ten, you commanded armies.*" This is an inscription of the year III. In fact, there are portraits of Rameses in a child's dress; the double crown is on his head, and he still carries his finger at his mouth, the symbol adopted to designate infancy.*

---

* At the Museum of the Louvre in Paris may be seen in case C, in the Historic Hall, on the first floor, two bas reliefs representing Rameses II. In one of them the prince is already a youth : he is standing near a lion, with a bow in his hand ; but he still wears the plait of hair, the distinguishing emblem that was laid aside on attaining manhood. In the other fragment, Rameses II., still a mere infant, is

III.

THE monuments, while they are silent with regard to the termination of Seti's reign, and his death, have transmitted to us details concerning the consecration ceremonial of the Pharaohs of his dynasty, which enable us, without making any great archaic efforts, to retrace the scene of his son's coronation. At the moment when the existing generation is dying out around us, while it looks on with coldness and mockery at the last essays of monarchy now dilapidated by time and deprived of credit by the progress of ideas, it may not prove uninteresting, perhaps, to see what it was at the outset in the ages of monarchic fervor and popularity. Nothing, it seems to us, enables one to appreciate the distance traversed so perfectly, as to reascend the stream of time, in fancy, to the period when society was in its youth, and the masses of men, well or ill conducted during their passage through life, rolled along inert, from the cradle to the tomb, in blind

---

nevertheless King, as the *urœus*, viper or *nazha*, which surmounts his crest, and the titles carved around him, bear witness. He wears the long dangling tress, and carries his finger at his mouth, as a token of childhood.

adoration of their guides; when human thought, shut up in the depths of the temples, had no other perception of the divine ideal than in objects of surprise and terror—the brutalities of matter in nature, and in humanity, the tyranny of Kings. When, after the 72 days of mourning prescribed by the funereal regulations, the corpse of Seti had been deposited in the magnificent tomb which he had prepared for himself *in the holy mountain of the West*,* beside the last resting places of the *other terrestrial gods*, his predecessors ; and when, by virtue of other consecrated rites, the moment for the establishment of his son Mei-Amoun upon the throne had been decided and proclaimed, Thebes, the city of Ammon, saw flowing in to her all the

---

* This tomb is that discovered and described by Belzoni. The Museum of the Louvre has a superb fragment of it, in No. 7 of the bas reliefs.

Most of the tombs of the valley of Biban-el-Moluk have remained unfinished, because, upon the death of the sovereigns who caused them to be excavated, the work ceased and the corpse was deposited and sealed in its resting-place in the condition in which the sepulchre happened to be at that moment.

There was no exception to this rule for any but Seti, Rameses Hikpun, and his son Rameses IV. The tomb of the great Mei-Amoun, destroyed, undoubtedly, by the Persians, has never been pointed out.—See Lenormand, *Musée des Antiq. égypt.*, p. 20.

functionaries of the two first classes who by right or through duty had a marked place in the *panegyrics*, or great public ceremonies.

The entrenched camps with which, in emulation of the ancient Hycsos camp of Wara, the Pharaohs of the eighteenth dynasty had covered their capital on both banks of the Nile, received, within their spacious enclosures, the deputations of the army sent from all the cantonments that maintained on the uttermost frontiers the integrity of the empire or the submission of the newly subjugated tribes. The rich dwellings which the great vassals had to keep up around the palace of their sovereign became peopled with Œris, intendants of the Egyptian nomes, or governors of conquered territories. These brought with them, mingling in their showy retinues, and laden with rich tribute, the chiefs of distant countries of the south who had been reduced to subordinate rank or positively conquered and made vassals. Many of the latter also were from the western region of the oases, or the shores of the Red Sea, and the Asiatic confines. In a word, the mysterious dwellings of the great Theban triad; the innermost retreats of the sacerdotal colleges were thrown open to give hospitality to the eponymic divinities of all the local religions of the valley of the Nile, which, borne in pomp along the river by their prophets, their pontiffs and their choristers, came to intercede respectfully with Ammon-Ra, *their lord and father,* in favor of the mortal who was to become *the guardian Sun* of justice among men.

IV.

ON the appointed day, so soon as the sun rising above the horizon of the Arabic chain, had gilded the opposite summits of the Libyan mountains, sanctified by the presence of the royal necropolis or city of the dead, and floods of sparkling light began to ripple along the masses of sandstone and marble, red porphyry and black or rose-colored granite which, reared in gigantic temples; hewn in the vast pylons; carved in obelisks; sculptured in sphinxes and colossi, seemed, at Thebes more than in the rest of Egypt, like the material envelope of the empire's mysterious soul, a tremendous clamor of human voices and instruments of music, rising from the bosom of the city, saluted the appearance of the Pelasgic god and gave the signal for the commencement of the day's ceremonies. All who were to take part in the latter hastened to range them-

Avenue of the Rams at Karnak (restored).

selves along the approaches to the palace where Mei-Amoun had passed, in seclusion, the period of his mourning. Under the main portico stood a magnificent *naos** upon supports of ebony carved in symbolical caryatides. It contained a throne of ivory, the base of which represented in gilded relief the sphinx, the emblem of wisdom united with strength, and the lion, the symbol of courage. Of this throne the colored statues of Tmei, the goddess of justice, and of Hor-Mœi, the sun-god of truth, with outstretched arms and expanded wings, formed the background and sustained the dais. The king, his forehead encircled with a simple band surmounted with a golden *uræus* set with jewels, having seated himself in this kind of case or shrine, twelve Oeris or warrior chieftains, the first in the empire in dignity and birth, uplifted him on their shoulders. Other great personages there took hold, each one of some particular part of the supports and steps leading to the throne, and all moved off together, preceded by an immense crowd, to the temple of Ammon.

The march was opened by a band of vocal and instrumental music in which figured the rudimentary types of the flutes, trumpets and drums still in

---

* A car or chair of state.

use. The members of the king's household and the functionaries of his home establishment came next, and immediately after them, the royal nacs surrounded by attendants, by fanbearers and young children of the sacerdotal caste carrying the sceptre, the arms and the other insignia of the monarch, before whom the first of the princes of the blood and the son of the high priest burned incense in golden censers.

The Queen Nofre-Ari, the youthful companion of Mei-Amoun when he too was young, robed like him in rich and almost transparent tissues, of which India even then possessed the secret, and like him displaying about her black waving masses of hair, and in the many ornaments of her neck, her arms and her naked feet all that was most precious among the pearls and corals of the Erythrean seas and the emeralds of the Troglodytes, accumulated during the lapse of centuries in the treasury of the Pharaohs, followed her spouse in an elegant palanquin, the elastic hammock of which, constructed of fine flax and gold, seemed suspended to stalks of rose-colored and blue lotus. Above it, a broad dais woven of the rainbow-hued spoils of the most brilliant birds of the Tropics, threw forth coruscating, ever-changing shades and tints.

Behind the Queen came on, in two parallel lines

An Egyptian Princess in her palanquin (according to Wilkinson).

the princes and princesses of the blood, the vassal kings, and the dignitaries of the priesthood and the army. Detachments of the latter, regularly drawn up in line by platoons under their respective officers and standards, terminated the procession which even the long avenue of sphinxes and rams,* leading from the banks of the river to the main entrance of the temple, could not wholly contain.

V.

In front of the sacred edifice of which the granite depths resounded with solemn and mysterious murmurs, the military music ceased, and the royal pageant halted.

The brazen gates, placed between two large pylons, gave passage to a long succession of priestly choirs advancing to the presence of Mei-Amoun, these were the local ecclesiastics of all the great temples in the Empire, and all the peculiar creeds of different places which time, conquest and the policy of legislators had made part of the system subordinate to Theban divinity. They brought the

---

* Colossal stone statues of rams were used like the sphinxes to adorn the avenues of the temples.

benedictions of their gods to the new son whom Ammon on that day adopted; nay more, they brought the gods themselves. *Baris* or barks sustained on the shoulders of groups of eighteen or twenty-four priests, according to the importance of the divine personage represented on the prow or the poop of each one of them, contained small *naos* or tabernacles carefully veiled with a thick tissue of silver and gold. There, hidden from the sight of every profane eye, were supposed to be stationed those renowned gods descended from the Vedic Aria upon the land of Kemi at successive and unknown epochs, viz: Ph-t-ah or Agny, meaning *fire;* Ph-Ra;* Jom; † Sevek; ‡ Asiri; § and those other local conceptions, half monster and half myth, which the pontiff teachers of Ethiopia had engrafted upon the coarse fetiches of the Cushites, the original inhabitants of the valley of the Nile, and which were all associated in divine families or households analogous to the great initial triad of Thebes.

As each *bari* filed along in its place in the proces-

---

* An equivalent of Re, Ra, Ri, La, El, the Sun.

† Om, Aom, Homa, the god of the Cup.

‡ Siva. § Asura. These were the Indian deities and titles with which the analogy of the Egyptian gods and goddesses is thus indicated.

sion, in front of Mei-Amoun the priests who carried it mingled praises of the King in their hymns, attributing to him all the virtues of which their particular deity was, more especially, the type, the inspiration or the symbol: some extolled his sense of justice and his magnanimity; others his hatred of falsehood and his love for the good; these sang laudations of his wisdom and his prudence and their control over his passions, and those his strength and courage in overcoming his enemies.*

VI.

THE tabernacles of the gods were followed by statuettes of the royal ancestors and predecessors of Mei-Amoun† also carried and interpreted by priests. Then, in the midst of another sacerdotal group, the white bull, the living emblem of Ammon-Ra, covered with flowers and enveloped in a cloud of incense, appeared on the threshold of the temple, as though to invite the new Aroeri to cross it.

Then, descending from his elevated *naos*, Mei-Amoun on foot proceeded through the interior

---

* See Diodorus, Book I., chapter 70.
† See Appendix VI.

porticoes and the high colonnades of the hypostylic halls toward the sanctuary where, upon an altar
of porphyry, sat the grand Theban triad. The
priestly choirs, the sacred *baris*, the images of the
ancestors, the royal family and the chiefs of the
Œris only went in thither with him.

On his arrival, the high priest presiding over the
pageant, caused the pontiffs officiating under him
to intone the chant consecrated to the Divine light
revealing itself to mortals. Standing erect at the
altar, he there received the King, who, ascending to
a place beside him, aided him in completing the
sacrifice ordained for the occasion; poured out
consecrated libations before Ammon; burned the
prescribed incense, amid a shower of flowers, and
prostrated himself while pronouncing these words,
at once so haughty and so simple:

"I come to my father Ammon at the end of the
procession of gods which he forever admits to his
presence."

During this time, these same gods and their terrestrial retinue wheeled solemnly around the altar,
mingling with the homage that they laid at the feet
of the King of Heaven, as they passed, the wishes
which they expressed for the welfare of the new
King of the Earth. The strange import of these
antique litanies may be conjectured from the

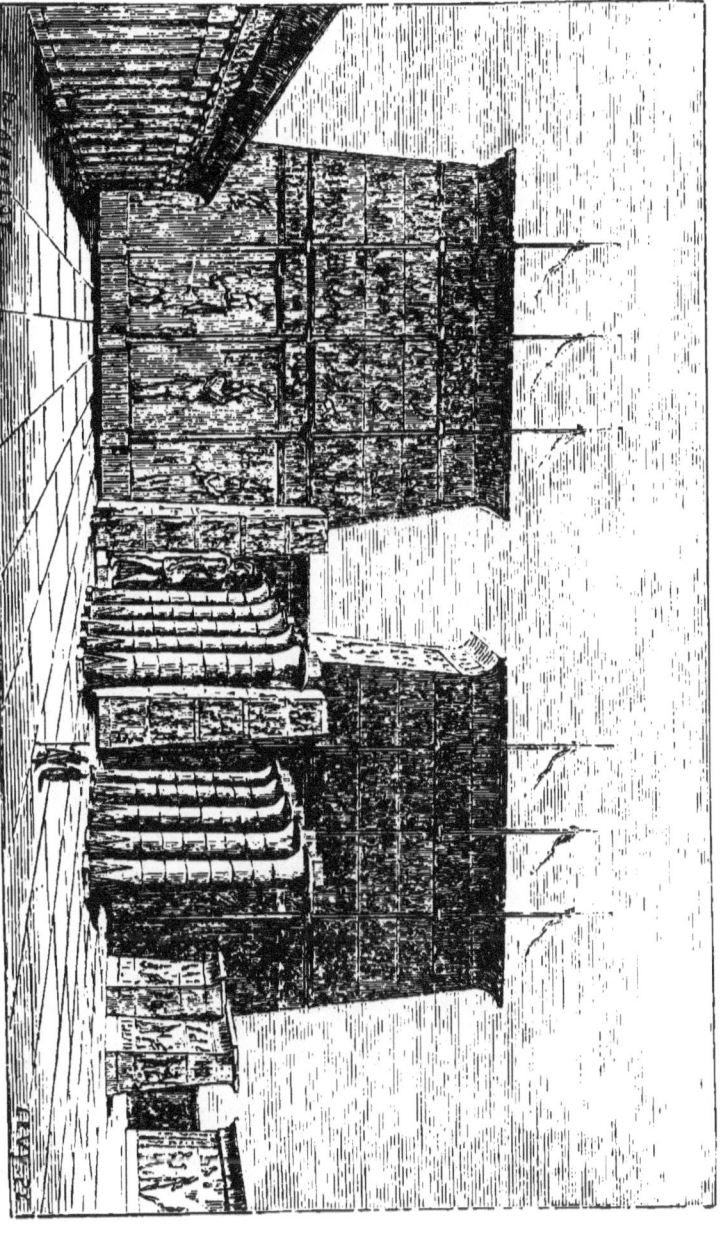

Karnak, the Interior Court (restored according to the Egyptian Commission).

following fragments which have been preserved for us by the mural inscriptions:

The Goddess Maut.
(The grand-mother and companion of Ammon.)

"I come to render homage to the sovereign of the gods, Ammon-Ra, the governing and controlling head of the land of Kemi, in order that he may grant long years to his son—King Rameses—who loves him."

The God Khons.
(Son of Maut and Ammon.)

"We approach thee, to serve thy Majesty, Oh, sovereign lord, Ammon-Ra! grant a pure and safely established life to thy son who loves thee,—Rameses, the lord of the Earth."

The Queen Nofre-Ari.

"And I, the royal spouse, the all-powerful mistress of the world, I bring my homage, also, to Ammon-Ra, King of gods and men. My heart rejoices in thy loving kindness; I leap with delight under the weight of thy favors. Oh thou who dost establish the seat of thy power in the dwelling of thy son, the lord of the world, Rameses, accord to him a firmly established and pure life. May his years be counted by periods of panegyrics."

VII.

To this series of prayers and intercessions, Ammon-Ra replies by the mouth of his high-priest speaking to Mei-Amoun: "My well-beloved son, receive from me a pure life and long days to pass upon the throne of Kemi. Thou shalt joyously control the world; Thoth has written down beside thy name all the royal attributes of the celestial Aroeri. The South and the North, the East and the West, shall be brought under thy yoke; all the good gates shall be opened to thee. I give the evil races to thee to trample beneath thy sandals. The force of thy arm shall triumph in all parts of the world, and the terror of thy name shall stamp itself deeply on the heaps of the barbarians. I give to thee, oh! my son, the scythe of battle to restrain the foreign nations, and to sever the heads of the impure. Take the whip and the sceptre to rule the land of Kemi. By my orders, the lady of the celestial palace has prepared for thee, the diadem of the sun. May this helmet remain upon thy forehead, where I place it, forever! . . . ."

At these words, Rameses having seized the crown upon the altar to place it on his head, the high priest stretched forth his pastoral staff toward the four quarters of the globe, and while the assistant pontiffs set at liberty four living geese which, kept in reserve until that moment, represented the genii of the four cardinal points of the compass, he exclaimed:

"Amset, Hapi Dawn-Mutef and Keba-snuf,
Go ye toward
The South, the North, the West, the East,
And tell the gods of those regions
That Horus, the son of Isis and of Asiri,
Has put the Pshent upon his forehead,
That King Rameses has put on the Pshent!"

His head encircled with this mystic tiara, Mei-Amoun had, then, to cut with his own hands a stalk of wheat which had grown within one of the enclosures of the temple, and to place it upon the altar of Ammon. This offering and the reading aloud by the high-priest of certain sealed rules relative to the duties and conduct of kings terminated the religious ceremony. Rameses was then escorted with the white bull and the images of the ancestral Kings, back to the exterior limits of the temple, and, amid a cloud of incense and flowers, regained the naos that was awaiting him in front of the pylons; then, preceded and followed with acclamations, oaths of fidelity and universal expressions of interest and regard, he advanced slowly to his palace, between two rows of sphinxes whose granite heads, that day adorned with ornaments and a royal or divine head-dress which determined the symbolical expression of each of them, seemed to become animated with the breath of human enthusiasm and rise up to salute the new sovereign as he passed by.

Such were the grand official pageants of Egypt fourteen centuries before Jesus Christ.

The Egyptian monarchs celebrated, during their entire reign, the anniversary of their coronation, by a ceremony of the same kind, less imposing no doubt than the first, but invested, by the events of the year, with more or less interest and distinction.

VIII.

Were the question to be asked, "What was the position of the *people* in these festivals?" and if that expression meant the plebeian throng of artisans, mechanics, laborers and soldiers, who to-day make up the living force of a nation, we should have to reply that the *people* did not exist in the Egypt of the Rameses, and that the day of their appearance and rise had not yet dawned upon any human community.

The Sphinx of Rameses II. (according to the Sphinx at the Louvre).

Below these two classes, one of which was the educating and the other the conquering caste in the valley of the Nile, there were crowds of artisans, of workers-by-hand who, under the direction of chiefs belonging to the religious castes, cut and built masonry; melted and worked with the metals; spun flax and *byssus;* in fine, toiled at the trades assigned to them, from the cradle, by law or by descent. There were farmers who tilled the lands given to them by the king, the priests or the warriors who were the sole owners of the soil of the empire. Upon the borders of the deserts, around the oases and the broad levels of the Delta, lived herdsmen who transmitted, from father to son, the business of raising and guarding the flocks and herds of the royal ecclesiastical or military domains. But these shepherds, these laborers, these artisans, excluded by law from public affairs; deprived, also, of the right to bear arms and of plying various trades at once; liable to be condemned, for each offence, to imprisonment, fines or the bastinado, that great resource of the stationary East, could not be looked upon as citizens, by modern eyes. Indeed, they do not appear to have differed much, upon the land of Kemi, from the Sudras of India to whom the **sovereign Master of things has assigned but one** office, viz., *that of serving the upper classes without depreciating their merits.**

Below them, again, were the slaves who had been purchased in the markets or captured in war.

IX.

This condition of things, which is not denied by the boldest admirers of the past history of Egypt, and is attested by the unanimous reports transmitted to us twenty centuries or more ago, by the sagacious observers of antiquity, who went from all the centres of civilization in those days, to the borders of the Nile to study a civilization older than their own—this state of things, we say, was discredited by one of our contemporaries as remarkable for the universality of his learning as for the vivacity of his scientific decisions. Arguing from the text of of some funereal inscriptions, in relation to the civil or private life of the ancient dwellers on the borders of the Nile, Mr. J. J. Ampère has felt authorized to declare that there never were castes among them.†

---

* Manava Shastra. Book First.

† In reference to castes in Egypt, see *Revue des Deux Mondes*, 15 Sept., 1848.

Without disputing the validity of the documents adduced by that savant; without inquiring whether they did not belong to periods of perturbation in Egyptian history, to times of trouble and strife, like those which preceded the eighteenth and followed the nineteenth dynasty; and especially to ages of decline, like those in which the last Rameses passed away, we shall confine ourselves to ascertaining, with Mr. Ampère himself, that if, at certain epochs of Egyptian history, the functions of judges, engineers, architects, chiefs of *nomes* and districts, seem to have been exercised indifferently by priests, or by warriors, and if by chance there was so little demarcation between these two aristocratic classes, the same person could, sometimes, accumulate sacerdotal, military and civil offices, the line of separation between them and the inferior classes always remained so broad that nothing could obliterate it—not even death. For the honors paid to ancestors in the tombs, the admission of their names into the funereal inscriptions do not appear to have ever ceased to be the exclusive privilege of members of the priesthood and the army.

It would be easy to prove that of the two terms of this proposition, the last affirms much more decidedly than the former one, the existence of castes. However that may be, we shall leave to any one who has studied in good faith, the nature of man and the affiliation of his social conceptions, the task of deciding whether deductions drawn from hieroglyphics, or from a doubtful interpretation and uncertain dates, are sufficient to refute the formal assertions of Herodotus, Plato, Strabo and Diodorus, who affirmed nothing concerning the institutions of Egypt without having seen them with their own eyes and touched them with their own hands.

For our part, even in the absence of such testimony, the contemplation of the valley of the Nile, which has been for 3000 years impotent in the production of a people, the sight of the degraded race that now occupies the homes of Thothmes III., of Seti and of Mei-Amoun, would have sufficed to convince us that this long hereditary lethargy, this stupor that has fallen there upon the growth of that progress of which Providence has planted the seed in the bosom of every region and every man, can be attributed to nothing but the violence of a rigid system of castes, too profoundly rooted into the land by conquest, and too long carried to extremes by the tyranny of established institutions.

X.

This point of historical criticism put aside, and we have touched upon it for no other purpose than to show how far one may go astray, in allowing oneself to be guided by epigraphy alone, we have to admit that the social ideal of our time could not have been that of ancient days. Civilization could not sustain itself, at the outset, and go on with its development excepting under the shelter of a rigorous system. There must be a coercive principle, material as well as moral, to compel wandering tribes, whether rude shepherds or savage hunters, to become a nation. The institution of castes promptly attained this end, in Egypt and India; but those who promoted it could not foresee how far their system, carried out to its ultimate results, would compromise the future. To the man of those days much less than to him who lives in our own time, was it given to uplift his gaze far enough toward the zenith to catch glimpes of the light reflected there from the dawn that still lingers below the horizon. He made up for this by creating according to the extent of his visual range and his requirements, a type of absolute monarchy in which the despot could be, up to a certain point, less the tyrant than the father of his subjects; wherein each class and each profession had its allotted sphere; wherein a religious dedication to the task, extending its influence from father to son, age after age, confined each individual within a circle of cares and duties amid which he was to live and die; wherein, finally, at the cost of beholding all human dignities concentrated upon a few heads, and the free will of each one sacrificed to the rigid mechanism of the law, the arts of peace, agricultural abundance, and commercial wealth seemed to diffuse themselves over the whole social body, at the hands of the sovereign like the blessings that descend from Divinity itself.* Some of the reigns of the eighteenth and nineteenth Egyptian dynasties, and, particularly, that of Rameses II., seem to have attained the limits of this ideal type.

---

* See Heeren "On the Commerce and Policy of the Ancients." Vol. I.

THE CAMPAIGNS OF RAMESES THE GREAT.

Situation, Wealth and Population of Egypt, on the Accession of Rameses.—The plausible Motives for his Expeditions.--Two Razzias at an Interval of Thirty-three Centuries.—Departure of Rameses for Asia.—His Army.—Testimony of Tacitus, Herodotus, Strabo and the Monuments.—A Bulletin of Victory, and a Poet Laureate of the Fourteenth Century before our Era. -The Battle of Atesh.—The return of Rameses.

I.

When Rameses ascended the throne, more than two centuries had elapsed since the expulsion of the Hycsos. The almost uninterrupted succession of a decade of memorable reigns had raised the internal prosperity of the empire, as well as its influence outside, to the highest pitch. The advantages resulting naturally from a long period of security; an administration equal to the needs of the epoch; the multiplication and good management of the canals, those peaceful conquerors of arable land won by them from the desert, were daily augmenting the chances of existence already so easy on a fertile soil and beneath a smiling sky. And, while all these causes combined were making the agricultural and industrial classes of Egypt the most laborious and the most compact population then existing, on the other hand, the military castes, trained to warfare from generation to generation by a series of successful distant expeditions, presented in its real effective force, and in that alleged in the exaggerated figures handed down to us by the writers of Greece and Rome,* the most martial, the best armed and the most formidable mass of combatants known to those ancient times.

Such elements of greatness, taken together with the youth of Mei-Amoun and his natural ardor, excited, as it was, in the highest degree by his first triumphs in war, and by the example of his father, render it needless for us to search, with the legendary historians, in the oracles of the gods or the interpretation of dreams, the motives of his ambition and his conquests.

---

* We cannot admit the 700,000 armed men spoken of in the recital of the Theban priests to Germanicus (See the *Annals* of Tacitus) any more readily than the picked force of 640,000 reported by Diodorus. Either of these accounts would make the numbers of the entire caste amount to from two to three millions of individuals, and that is excessive. See Appendix VII.

Moreover, at that time, great disorders were agitating the East, and the noise of their distant tumults could not but re-echo as far as the borders of the Nile. In the great irruptions that Seti I. had guided toward Central Asia, he had repeatedly come into collision with the confederation of the Khetas, in whose title seem to lie concealed both that of the old Hycsos and the more modern name of the Scythians. From the gorges of the Taurus and the Lebanon mountains, where they had established their citadels and the centre of their power, these ancient wandering races presided over the great movements of the Oriental populations which the religious or social convulsions of Upper Asia were incessantly detaching from the antique Aryan throne, and continually recruited their numbers with fresh swarms.

There was reason to apprehend that, ere long, all these torrents of men would follow the descending channel worn for them by former migrations, and, like them, pour down and inundate Egypt. To await their attacks was dangerous. It was better to hasten to meet them and to hurl them back toward the sources whence they came, or, at all events, to break the force of the stream, and scatter its ramifications over the earth. Thus, no doubt, thought Mei-Amoun, and from the modern point of view, we cannot but agree with him.

According to Diodorus, whom, we think, we can take for our guide in this matter, Mei-Amoun prepared himself for his great enterprise by such acts as were most likely to give his popularity deep root in the minds of his subjects. In order to feel assured of the fidelity of those whom he was to leave behind him on the soil of his country, and to make certain of the indomitable perseverance of the companions in arms selected to follow him, he strove to link them to his destiny by the ties of interest and of gratitude. Affable and cordial with all, he displayed a liberality equal to his unlimited power. He overwhelmed some with gifts; to others he distributed lands, while to still others, again, he remitted the fines and penalties they had incurred, and gave liberty to all prisoners of State, and all who had been incarcerated for debt, of whom the multitude then overstocked the jails.*

The population and area of the Empire increasing from reign to reign, and necessitating a new territorial division, he fixed the number of *nomes* or provincial governments† at thirty-six, and placed at the head of each, to preside over the local ad-

---

* See Diodorus, Book I.

† M. Brougsch, who very naturally, will have it that this administrative division of Egypt dates back to a period

ministration and the collection of taxes, men whose reputation or hereditary attachment to his dynasty recommended them the most to his confidence. One of the first results of this scheme having been an exact census of the military caste, he was enabled to raise from its midst an army composed of men who were the most robust and the most capable of supporting the long fatigues and perilous chances of distant or unknown climes. He gave them for leaders the playmates of his childhood and the comrades who had shared the exploits of his early youth. All of them, like himself, full of ardor and ambition and inured to warlike exercises, were bound to each other by fraternal ties of which the common bond was an absolute devotion to Mei-Amoun, who, at the expense of the treasures amassed by his ancestors, and the regions annexed to the domains of the crown by previous conquests, had provided for their pecuniary welfare sufficiently to leave them free from any other anxieties than those of war.*

---

much anterior to Rameses, raises the number of nomes to forty-four, equally divided between Upper and Lower Egypt. He confesses, however, that concerning *many nomes* of this latter part of the Egyptian territory, he still felt some lingering uncertainty, the solution of which demands fresh researches and discoveries.

* Diodorus Book I, ch. LIV.

II.

After having thus regulated the organization of the interior, and of the army, Mei-Amoun had still to provide for the security of the frontiers during the whole period of his projected absence, on his distant expeditions. On the western side, his possession of the oases, maintained by fortified posts, and the immensity of the desert, dispelled the idea of all serious danger. On the north, the carefully secured and guarded locks and barriers that closed the seven mouths of the Nile, sufficed to prevent the rovers of the Mediterranean from penetrating into Egypt, and the natives from leaving it. The Isthmus of Suez, the point of both departure and arrival for all the Asiatic routes, and partly covered by the *Bitter Lakes* which, at the epoch in question, every high tide still put in communication with the neighboring gulf, was moreover sheltered from all attack by the numerous military establishments that were to serve as a base for the warlike operations toward the East that Rameses was planning. There remained the districts on the south, ever exposed to the descents of the savage hordes belonging to *the bad race* of Cush, and the *Sea-Weed Lake*, the way to which the monsoons of the Indian Ocean had taught to the Pelasgians from the banks of the

Indus and the Nerbudda. Always in quest of adventure and pillage, as their brethren of the Ægean Sea and of the open Ocean were to be, after an interval of many centuries, they frequently came thither to gather booty, sometimes as traders but oftener as pirates.

To remedy this double inconvenience, two things seemed necessary to Mei-Amoun;—the subjugation of Upper Ethiopia and the establishment of a military marine which, riding supreme on the waters of the Arabian Gulf, should, in maintaining the security of the two shores, guarantee the communications that trade and the working of the copper mines on the peninsula of Tor had kept open between them for several centuries. These two enterprises were interlinked, because the soil of Egypt and of Lower Nubia lacking timber fit for naval construction, it was necessary to seek that material upon the broad plateaux watered by the tributaries of the great river above Meroe.

Consequently, he penetrated those regions and traversed them in every direction, at the head of a continually victorious army, exacting tribute in gold, ivory, ebony, and building-timber from all the Ethiopian tribes extending from the Nile to the Red Sea, who, until then, had escaped the Egyptian yoke.

Then, when the shipyards established in the ports subsequently named Adulis, Berenice and Leucos * had given him the first *long vessels* constructed by Egyptian hands,† he embarked upon the waters of the Arabian Gulf, and subdued its islands, and its shores as far as its southern extremity. The port of Mosselycus, situated not far from Cape Guardafui, and six hundred leagues from Thebes was, according to Pliny and Strabo, the extreme point reached by Rameses in that direction.‡

The mementoes of these events, precursors as they were of others on a grander scale, may still be deciphered on the ruins that cover Mount Barkal to the south of Nubia, as also among the broken remains of the Rameseum or great temple of Thebes, on the right bank. In one of the bas relief pictures of the *speos* of Ipsamboul, even the triumphal entry of Rameses into his capital, on his return from the regions of the south, has been made out.

Helmet on head, encased in a coat of mail, and erect in a superb chariot drawn by four magnificently caparisoned horses, the Egyptian hero, amid the acclamations of his soldiers, is driving before

---

* Herodotus, Book II.
† Diodorus, Book I. ch. lv.
‡ Strabo, Book LVI. Pliny Book VI.

him a throng of negro and Leuco-Ethiopean captives with which he is going to *do homage* to the Theban triad.

What meaning must we assign to this terrible expression? Egyptian scholars refuse to see anything in it but the right which war gave to the master over his slave, to the victor over the vanquished, without admitting that this right was ever extended so far as to cover human sacrifice. But those who do not, without some restrictions, ascribe very pure or very exalted light to the Egyptian priesthood; those who remember what pitiless hatred to the foreigner Egypt bequeathed to all the races that inherited either her blood or her doctrines, and what unworthy trophies the warriors of the Nile sought out with frantic eagerness on the battle-field; all, in fine, who acknowledge the fifteenth, sixteenth and twenty-second verses of the first book of Exodus to be historical documents, will, no doubt, think with us that, in the period we describe, the prisoner of war had but feeble guarantees against *bloody oblation*, and the treatment meted out to the condemned, in the philanthropy of the priests of Egypt, the generosity of her warriors and the gentleness or the clemency of her kings.*

---

* A carved pillar of the reign of Amenoph II., lately found in the temple of Amada in Nubia, unfortunately brings

III.

ONE of the bas-reliefs of Beit-el-Wally shows us Mei-Amoun seated in a brilliant *naos* and causing a long procession, the immediate result of his victories in Ethiopia, to file before him. There are groups of prisoners, among whom figures an Amenoph, the chief ruler of that part of the land of Cush which the inscriptions designate as *bad;* tables and sideboards covered with gold-dust and golden rings; logs of ebony wood, elephant tusks, ostrich feathers and leopard skins—all those articles of luxury and rarity, in fine, which the nations of the north and the east have never ceased, since the time in ques-

---

terrible confirmation to the hints we have expressed. Its precise language is this : "After having vanquished his enemies, and enlarged the frontiers of Egypt, his *Holiness* Amenoph II.) came back from the country of the Upper Ruteni (Upper Assyria) and filled the heart of his father, Ammon-Ra, with joy; for he had, with his own war-club, *massacred* seven kings captured in the city of Tashis and led in chains on board of his vessel. Six of these kings, after having had their hands cut off, were hung opposite to the pylons of Thebes.

"As for the other enemy, he was conveyed by water to Nubia, and hung to the wall of the city of Napata, to display to *the evil races of Cush* the victories won by his majesty over all the nations of the world, and the manner in which he chastises them."

tion, to bear away from Africa, that mother of gold, of slaves and of monsters whose deplorably prolific yield four thousand years of pillage have not been able to exhaust.

The names of some of the tribes subjugated in this expedition have their analogous equivalents on the modern map of Abyssinia and Sennaar; unfortunately, this similarity of names is not the only one that may be traced between those whom Mei-Amoun conquered, and their descendants living in our own day.

It is well known that the present chiefs of the Eastern Soudan country annually organize murdering and robbing expeditions—*ghrazias* or razzias as they term them—against the inhabitants of the higher levels of the central table-land of Africa. Then, too, the narratives that modern travellers give of these acts of plunder sound like a faithful translation of the legends explaining one of the bas-reliefs of Beit-el-Wally destined to transmit to posterity the remembrance of a raid directed by Rameses against the Nahazis, the ancestors of the negroes of the present day.

According to the hieroglyphic recital legible there, " The barbarians, utterly routed, are flying in consternation before the Egyptian hero, who is pursuing them in a chariot, at furious speed, and reaches them with his arrows even in the shelter of their forests. Men, women, children and greybeards, terrified at the sight of the carnage, are vainly endeavoring to escape extermination, and to find a refuge in retreats that they share with the wild beasts."*

In connection with this picture, read another description sketched but yesterday, nearly on the same spot, and in which the descendants of the same hostile races figure:

"The Abyssinian army had furiously pursued the wretched tribe of Soddo-Gallas, and their horsemen had soon overtaken a crowd of old men, women and children unable to escape. The sight of these unfortunate people, far from awaking in them that sentiment of compassion so natural to us when we behold helpless feebleness, only served to excite their brutal instinct for bloodshed. Some of them came back with their bleeding trophies paraded in the most indecent manner, and vaunted their exploits in obscene recitals; others brought with them the wives and daughters of the helpless wretches whom they had massacred or mutilated. It was but one long wail of grief and despair.

---

* Champollion's Letters written from Egypt and Nubia.—Cherubini's Nubia. Firmin Didot

Royal Scribes registering Negro and Asiatic Prisoners.

When the army pressed forward in the direction of a thicket where the Gallas, it was supposed, had taken refuge, I withdrew, so as not to witness the slaughter of the poor creatures who, to escape the javelins hurled at them, were clambering up into the trees. There they were shot like sparrows, and thither, also, came the king, who would not have missed a humming-bird, at blank range, to bring down a miserable fugitive from the covert of the branches where he had tried to hide himself."*

Between these two narratives thirty-three centuries had elapsed, sweeping away the Pharaohs and their empire, along with the nations that replaced them on the stage of the world and the gods that dethroned their gods. All the races who owned submission to Horus, the divine shepherd of men, have, turn by turn, seized and borne the sceptre of civilization and renewed the face of the Earth. The Nahazis form the sole exception. Cast outside of the track of the great migrations; fastened to a harsh and enervating soil, under a sky of brass, they remained motionless, in their barbarism, their ignorance, and their native weakness and terror; having no other relations with the remaining members of the great family than such as the

---

* Chas. Lefèvre's Journey to Abyssinia, vol. ii., pp. 245, 246.

wild animals of their forests hold with the hunter, they have for five thousand years paid to them tribute of flesh and blood, and seen the bones of their children scattered to all the four quarters of the globe, along the roads that lead to every slave mart. Gloomy fate! unjustifiable in every age, but especially so in ours, when civilization, grown up and triumphant, no longer needs, as it did in the time of the Rameses, to secure its cradle against the assaults of barbarism, and has ceased to be, for any nation, a privileged deposit, the jealous safe-keeping of which implies, as the first of social duties, hatred, war and oppression for the stranger.

IV.

THE preceding facts must have fully occupied the first two years of the reign of Mei-Amoun, and it was probably only toward the beginning of the third that, having provided for all that the accomplishment of his vast designs demanded, and having confided the government of Egypt to the Queen, assisted by a council of regency, he set in movement for the conquest of Asia the masses which he had accumulated with that intent on the borders of the Isthmus.

Egyptian Cavalry.

If the monuments have not placed it in our power to correct the assertions of the ancients with regard to the numerical strength of that army, they at least leave us in the way to compensate for the silence that they have maintained with regard to the material of which it was composed.

The cavalry of our modern armies was represented in it, as it continued to be for a long time afterward by squadrons of war-chariots manned by the flower of the Œris.* The rest of the military caste furnished the *hoplites* or troops of the line on foot, who, protected by a cuirass and shielded by a buckler, used the lance, the sword and the battle-axe in combat, and manœuvred, according to prescribed rules, eight or ten men deep. Then, there was the light infantry, whose duty it was to reconnoitre and clear the roads, to skirmish in the advanced guard, and to cover, with its cloud of archers and slingers, the wings of the army and the intervals between the chariots. It probably recruited among the auxiliary tribes on the frontiers, and from the Ethopian allies its numerous soldiers

---

* The number of these chariot teams, each consisting of two horses at least, indicates clearly the importance and the degree of development which the business of raising and training that noble race of animals had assumed in the few generations that had elapsed since their introduction on the borders of the Nile.

who, armed with all the projectile weapons known at that period, held also in reserve for hand to hand struggles that terrible battle scythe or sickle, the murderous use of which has been perpetuated to this day in Africa, among the Abyssinians and the Gallas, and in Asia, among the Ghoorkas of the Himalayas and of the Western Ghauts.

All these troops performed their evolutions to the sound of the trumpet and the drum, under the banners of their respective chiefs; but above all these special and subordinate symbols, there rose at the extremity of a tall and strong staff, the ensign of the Empire, all glittering with the splendor of pure and massive gold. It consisted of a ram's head surmounted with the solar disk, the double symbol of Ammon-Ra leading his worshippers against the hostile races. Borne along on a magnificent chariot, which had to be kept close to that of the sovereign, under all circumstances, this venerated emblem, indicated to the gaze of all,—on the march, and in actual battle,—the centre of the army and the presence of its leader,—and when in camp, the position of the royal pavilion.

V.

FROM the borders of the Nile to those of the Tigris, Rameses could follow routes upon which nearly all his predecessors, dating from Thothmes I., had left some land-marks. Since the opulent Pentapolis of the Jordan had sunk in the bituminous gulf of the Dead Sea, the most compact centres of permanent population, existing between Egypt and upper Asia, were the maritime establishments which the Cushites of Canaan, driven from the shores of the Erythrean gulfs by convulsions of the soil, had founded upon the Syrian coast; the fortified cities which the Khetas had built between the Orontes and the Euphrates, and, lastly, Babel in the land of Shinar, where a celebrated temple of the Sun and a great navigable river, attracted caravans and flotillas of pilgrims and traders from all directions.

To the eastward of the Naharain country—Naharaina-Kah on the Ipsamboul inscriptions, meaning Mesopotamia,—rise the mountainous regions, that, at a later period, were to form the nucleus of the empires of Semiramis and Cyrus. Here, for Rameses, the realm of the unknown began, and an entire new world opened before him, in which he, undoubtedly, had no other guide than the instinctive hatred against the men of the Northeast that animated his army, and the fugitive currents of the tribes and races with which he came into collision as he passed on.

Nevertheless, one may infer from the narrations on this subject which the ancients have left to us, separating them from the exaggerations credited by Diodorus, that the march of the Egyptian conqueror, at first directed eastward, touched, perhaps, on the Hindoo Koosh and Bactrian country, and then diverging toward the north, turned back again by a long elliptical curve and debouched upon the European shores of the Propontis. Thus, Rameses II. after having left the imprint of his feet upon the rocks of Cape Guardafui, could, after an interval of some years, cause images of himself to be graven on the mythical terraces of the Indian Parnassus, and appear in the semblance of a fearful and unknown god to the savages inhabiting the shores of the Thracian Bosphorus. We must run down along the lists of chronology more than ten centuries in order to again find in the son of Philip so indefatigable a promoter of the mixture of races, and the diffusion of ideas.

When Germanicus, one of the latest heroes of antique society in its decline, for whom Rome wept bitterly and whom Tacitus extolled, repaired to the

Egyptian Infantry (according to the monuments)

East where a premature death awaited him, he visited the vast remains of Thebes in sober meditation, and, having asked one of the priests then present, a living relic in the midst of so many ruins, the meaning of the sacred characters that covered the edifices still standing, the latter replied while he interpreted the inscriptions, that the King Rameses, at the head of an army of 700,000 men, had subjugated Libya and Ethiopia, the country of the Medes and Persians, Bactria and Scythia; that he had brought under the yoke of his empire, the countries inhabited by the Syrians and the Armenians, Cappadocia, which is near to them, and all hither Asia from the Sea of Bithynia to that of Lycia.*. . .

VI.

Herodotus, who preceded Germanicus by more than 450 years on the borders of the Nile, and Tacitus by at least five centuries in history, likewise reports, in accordance with the statement of the priests, that Sesostris (Rameses II.), after the sub-

---

* See the *Annals* of Tacitus, Book II., chap. lx.

jugation of Ethiopia, marched with a numerous army to the conquest of Asia, and subdued all the nations he encountered on the way, taking care, after each victory, to erect landmarks upon which inscriptions narrated the details of the combat, the name of his country and his own. . . . . Thus traversing the continent, he passed from Asia into Europe, and subdued the Thracians and Scythians; "but I do not think," adds the historian, "that he penetrated any farther in that direction, for, although we find among the last named nations the trophies that he set up, none are discovered beyond their confines."

"Retracing his steps, he halted on the banks of the Phasis; but I do not make out clearly whether it was voluntarily that he left a part of his army there to colonize the country; or whether detachments of his soldiers, fatigued and exhausted by their long marches, settled there in spite of him. . . . .

"However that may be, it appears positive that the Colchians are of Egyptian origin. I suspected this fact; others had mentioned it to me, and I wished to make certain of it for myself. I can affirm that the two nations have retained remembrances of each other, which are much more vivid, however, among the Colchians than among the Egyptians.

Bass-Relief of Sesostris near Sardis, from a photograph.

. . . These nations both have a black skin and woolly hair . . . practise circumcision; live in the same manner; cultivate and work flax in the same style; in fine, *speak the same language.*' Herodotus adds that most of the monuments which Sesostris had caused to be set up in commemoration of his victories had already ceased to exist, in his day; but that he had, with his own eyes, seen as many as three,—which have been found in our time, at the places pointed out; one in Syrian Palestine and the other two in Ionia, on the roads from Ephesus to Phocæa and from Smyrna to Sardis. "Each one of these, carved in relief on a wall of rock, represents a warrior five cubits in height. holding a javelin in his right hand, and in his left a bow. The rest of his equipment is equally Egyptian and Ethiopian. On his breast, he bears an inscription in sacred characters, to this purport: "*It is I who have conquered this country by the strength of my arm.*"*

Strabo, whose birth in Asia Minor and long journeys in the East gave him the opportunity to verify or correct with his own eyesight the assertions of *the father* of history, declares that the routes followed by Rameses-Sesostris had been det-

---

* Herodotus, Book II., chaps. 102, 103, 104, 105.

ted with commemorative columns, inscriptions, bas-reliefs and temples.*

The great historical pages of Ipsamboul, Luxor and Karnak confirm in most of their details, without invalidating any, the preceding attestations of the two great historians of Greece and Rome, and of the erudite geographer of Amasia; only that one must not expect to find in these monumental inscriptions the ethnical data of the nations and empires enumerated in the text of those writers. The ethnography of the days of Rameses transmitted but very few names to those of the Hellenic and Roman epochs. If appellations like Luki and Naharain may be easily translated in them by "Lycians" and "Mesopotamia," the wandering tribes of Arabia figure there only as the *children of the red soil:* the Rotenians hold the place afterward occupied by the Assyrians; Sengar is the name of the country of Babel, and in the regions where the empires of Media and Persia were to be reared, the Remeni, the Moshaushs and the Robus † range themselves along from north to south, between the Caspian Sea and the Ocean. Then, farther on, beyond that zone, in the vanguard

---

* Strabo. Book XVII.
† See Appendix VIII.

of the East, the offensive designation of *the plague of Kheta* marks out upon an immense space not limited toward the north, the numberless and warlike nomadic hordes which, since the days of the Hycsos, had supplied the most implacable enemies known to the warriors of the borders of the Nile.

It is not without some emotion that the historian records these names, effaced so many centuries ago from the memory of mankind; but especially is it not without profound interest that, amid these forgotten generations, which however took part, according to their gifts and opportunities, in the humanitary task of their period, he is enabled to ascertain the presence of the ancestors of a people who, after having long held the sceptre of antique civilization, have arisen before our eyes from the tomb in which the ages had buried them, to claim a place among the modern nations. It will be understood that we are here referring to the *Iouni*, evidently identical with the *Javans* of the Hebrew books, and the Yavanas of the Hindoos, whose tribes, scattered and floating about over Western Asia after their expulsion from Ariawarta, their original country, undoubtedly owed to their invasion by Rameses Mei-Amoun, to their struggles with that conqueror and their flight before his victorious armies, their concentration in the region surrounding the Ægean Sea, and thereby, too, the germ of their long subsequent history.

This double fact of an ancient antagonism in the heart of Asia, between the forefathers of the Greeks and the warriors of the Nile, and of the alliance of the former with the ancestors of the Medes and Persians, would no doubt have awakened singular incredulity among the contemporaries of Themistocles or Plato. Nevertheless, it has been repeatedly affirmed by Champollion, who, in the inscriptions at Karnak and in the Rameseum existing side by side, with the names of barbarous nations, in northern costumes, with shaven heads or their hair raised in a single lock or wisp like that of the "Red Skins" of America or the Mongols of Asia, declares that he read the title of these *Iouni* whose blue eyes and golden hair * Homer was to celebrate some ages later.

---

* This version of the illustrious Egyptian scholar is sustained by Messrs. Birch and Lepsius, who think that they have again come across the same name of a nation which they spell Ya-bu-na in the inscriptions attributed by them to the 12th and 13th dynasties.

VII.

For Champollion, the Khetas were Scythians; but M. de Rougé, followed by all the Egyptian scholars of the present day, considers them no other than the Chets or Hittites of the Bible, whose powerful confederation comprised, in the time of Rameses, a portion of Mesopotamia and the whole north of Syria on the two slopes of the Lebanon.

Whoever coincides with the ideas that we have advanced in the preceding pages, in reference to the Scythians of Justinus and T. Pompeius, will consider the difference of opinion existing, on this point, between the founder of Egyptian research and his worthiest successor, as reducing itself to a mere ethnical question, the same thing being transcribed in two different idioms.

A formidable revolt of the Asiatic tribes summoned Rameses into the midst of their encampments in the fifth year of his reign. In following the steps of the conqueror thither, we have unerring guides. The historical pictures dedicated to this campaign adorn a great number of monuments; they moreover comprised the first bulletin of victory that history has picked up. Besides, M. de Rougé has analyzed or translated them, here and there, with his usual penetration, in a special paper from which we borrow the following passages:

" While studying the battles represented in these mural paintings, says the learned and conscientious philologist, my attention was attracted by a singular episode in which the personal valor of the King seems to have extricated him from great peril: hence, too, it is repeated, as though by emulation, in the paintings of all the temples. Twice given in the Rameseum, it is also found at Luxor, at Ipsamboul and at Beit-el-Wally. In addition to the bulletin of the campaign reproduced by these bas-reliefs, a manuscript which Champollion has made famous in science, the papyrus of Sallier, now belonging to the British Museum, has preserved for us the greater part of a poem composed at the very period of the battle by a writer of the court of Rameses named *Penta-ur*. Champollion appears to have copied only a few lines of this manuscript nevertheless, his great knowledge of the Egyptian texts, revealed to him, as by instinct, the extremely interesting character of this document. He recognized in it the characteristics of a historical poem, and gathered from it, at the outset, the names of the hostile tribes in league with the Prince of Kheta. But, neither Champollion nor his successors had discerned the real theme of this epic frag-

Asiatic Races, hostile to the Egyptians (from the monuments).

ment, to wit : the great peril to which Rameses was exposed, when separated from his army and attacked, with his feeble escort, by a picked force consisting of twenty-five hundred chariots. This is the characteristic trait that enabled me to recognize the same incident carved on all the temples. The poem of Pen-ta-ur was esteemed by his contemporaries, for it had the distinguished honor to be carved upon one of the walls of Karnak, which it completely covered. It is too much defaced, at the present day, to serve for the completion of the manuscript; but the number of the columns formerly filled with hieroglyphics leads us to conjecture tha at least the first third part of the poem is lacking.

The historian may fill this deficiency, to some extent, by the aid of the official bulletins of the campaign, which the pictures of Ipsamboul and the Ramesseum have preserved almost intact; they will explain to us by what stratagem the hostile leader had succeeded in cutting off the Pharaoh and his retinue from the bulk of his army.

But I must first give notice that we are not as yet able to exactly determine the locality of the occurrence. The tribes of Mesopotamia figure with those of Syria in the confederation commanded by the Prince of Kheta; the city of Atesh, near which the fight took place, was the strongest post in the control of those tribes; the Egyptian armies moved via the north of Syria to reach the country in question, and the city was washed by a river called the Aranta. This name naturally recalls that of the Orontes, the only river of importance in Syria; yet this is all that we can say, at present, with regard to the position of a place that underwent several sieges, beheld bloody battles fought under its walls, and seems to have been the culminating point of the earliest struggles made, in those primitive times, for the mastery of the world."

"Such are the facts that stand forth from the story of the campaign as it is found carved at Ibsamboul and in the Rameseum.

"In the fifth year of his reign, on the ninth day of the eleventh month, (Epiphi,) Rameses was in Asia with his army, marching against the insurgent tribes commanded by the prince of Kheta. The king was advancing to the southward of the city, but he lacked information concerning the position of the hostile army, when some Bedouins came in to offer their services, and told him that the prince of Kheta, intimidated by the Egyptian advance, had retired toward the south, in the direction of the Khirab country. But these rovers were emissaries of the foe, specially entrusted with the task of misleading the Egyptians by their false reports. The confederates had really massed their forces secretly to the northward of Atesh. Rameses, thus deceived, moved to the northwestward of that city, and drew near to the enemy. At this juncture, his scouts brought in to him two other Kheta spies, who, after being severely bastinadoed, confessed that they had been sent to examine the position of the Egyptian army, and that all the confederate forces were concentrated behind the city of Atesh watching the movements of the Pharaoh for an opportunity to attack him at advantage.

"Rameses calls his generals together; reprimands them sternly for their lack of vigilance, and informs them that the Prince of the Khetas, uselessly pursued toward the south, by the Egyptian army, is there under the walls of Atesh ready to precipitate himself upon them. The generals acknowledge their delinquency, and that of the leaders of the scouts, who had obtained no information concerning the enemy's movements. An officer is then despatched in hot haste, to the main body of the army which is pursuing its march to the southward, thus uncovering the position of the king more and more.

"While this council of war is being held, the Prince of Kheta causes his troops to advance rapidly to the southward of Atesh, and long before the

Egyptian army has time to retrace its steps, the little band of followers and attendants who accompany the king is dispersed, and Rameses finds himself surrounded by the hostile chariots."*

It is into the midst of this critical phase of the action that what remains of the poem of Penta-ur transports us. The papyrus, worn and rent in many places, as it is, exhibits many a gap; and we confess, with all humility, that we have endeavored to supply some of its deficiencies by the help of the notes that Champollion has left, in reference to the same subject.†

VIII.

EXTRACTS FROM THE SALLIER PAPYRUS.

THE prince of Kheta came with his archers and his horsemen well armed; every chariot bore three men. They had gathered together the swiftest warriors of those base Khetas, carefully armed . . . . and had placed themselves in ambush to

---

* See the Vicomte Em. de Rougé's Memoir on the Campaigns of Sesostris, *Revue Contemporaine*, August, 1856.

† The reader will recognize these fragments by the mark which we have placed before and after them.

the northwest of the city of Atesh. They attacked the soldiers of the king when the sun, god of the two horizons, was at the middle of his course: the latter were on the march, and were not expecting an attack. The archers and the horsemen of his Majesty fell back before the enemy, who was master of Atesh on the left bank of the Aranta. . . . . Then his Majesty, strong and sound in constitution, rising like the god Month, put on the panoply of battle: arrayed in his weapons he was like unto Baal in his hour. The mighty coursers of his Majesty (*strength in Thebais* was their name) came forth from the grand stables of the Sun, the lord of justice, Rameses Mei Amoun.*

The king, rushing forth in his chariot, plunged into the ranks of the despicable Kheta: he was alone, no other near him. This onset his Majesty made in sight of his whole retinue. He found himself surrounded on all sides by two thousand five hundred swift chariots, manned by the bravest warriors of the pitiful Kheta and his numerous allies: *Aradus*, *Masu*, *Patasa*, *Kashkash*, *Œlon*, *Gazwatan*, *Khirab*, *Aktar*, *Atesh* and *Raka*. Each of

---

* The Louvre Museum (Historical Hall, case G) possesses a golden ring of singular shape, representing, on its collet, two tiny horses in relief. It may be that in them we behold a souvenir of the two steeds of Rameses II., who consecrated them to the Sun on his first return from Egypt.

their chariots bore three men . . . . and the king had with him neither his princes, nor his generals, nor the captains of the archers or of the chariots.

And this is what his Majesty of the sound and strong life said:

"What, then, is the intent of my father Ammon? Is it a father who would deny his son? Or have I trusted to my own thoughts? Have I not walked according to thy word? Has not thy mouth guided my goings forth, and thy counsels have they not directed me?" . . .

"Have I not dedicated to thee magnificent festivals in great number, and have I not filled thy house with my booty? There is building to thee a dwelling for myriads of years. . . . The whole world is gathering together to dedicate its offerings to thee. I have enriched thy domain; I have sacrificed to thee thirty thousand oxen, with all the scent-bearing herbs and choicest perfumes. . . . I have built for thee upon the sand, temples of blocks of stone; and bringing obelisks from Elephantina, I have reared eternal shafts in thy honor. For thee, the great ships toss upon the deep; they bear to thee the tribute of the nations. Who will say that like things have been done at any other time? Ignominy to him who resists thy designs; felicity

Rameses in Battle, from a bass-relief near Ipsamboul.

to him who understands thee, oh, Ammon! I invoke thee, oh, my father! I am in the midst of a throng of unknown tribes, and I am alone, before thee; no one is with me. My archers and my horsemen deserted me when I called aloud to them; not one among them hearkened to me when I cried to them for help. But I prefer Ammon to thousands of archers, to millions of horsemen and to myriads of young men arrayed in phalanx. The wiles of men are as naught; Ammon will prevail over them. Oh Sun! have I not obeyed the order of thy lips, and thy counsels have they not guided me? Have I not given glory to thee, to the ends of the Earth?"

These words resounded in Hermonthis; Phra comes to him who calls upon him; he stretches forth his hand to him. Rejoice and be glad . . . he flies to thee, he flies to thee . . . Rameses Mei-Amoun! He says to thee, "Behold, I am near thee; I am thy father, the Sun; my hand is with thee, and I am more, for thee, than millions of men arrayed together. It is I who am the lord of troops and armies, loving courage; I have found thy heart firm in valor, and my heart exults thereat."

When my master of the horse saw that I remained surrounded by so many chariots, he faltered, and his heart gave way for fear; a mighty terror seized on all his limbs. He said, then, to his Majesty: "My good master, generous King, sole protector of Egypt in the day of battle, we are tarrying alone in the midst of the foe; halt in thy course and let us save the breath of our lives. What can we do, oh, Rameses Meiamoun! my good master?"

And thus did his Majesty reply to his master of the horse:

"Have courage! strengthen thy heart, oh my comrade! I will plunge into their midst like the hawk from on high darting down upon his foe; hurled to the ground and slain, they shall roll in the dust. What does thy heart then think of these *Aamus?* Ammon . . . . would not be a god, did he not make glorious my countenance in the presence of their countless legions."

The king pierced his way into the army of these vile Khetas; six times did he enter into their midst. . . . . "I pursued them like Baal, in the hour of his might, and I slew them so that none could escape.

"I threw myself upon them, like unto the god Month; in a moment's space, my hand mowed them down. I slaughtered among them: I killed in their midst, and I was alone to shout aloud. there was no second word, not one of them lifted up his voice. Sutekh, the great warrior-Baal, was in all his members. . . . Each one of all my enemies felt his hand without strength against mine; they could no longer hold the bow or the spear.

The king, rallying around him the generals and the horsemen of his retinue, said to them: "Your comrades have not satisfied my heart; is there one among them who has deserved well of my country? If your lord had not arisen in his might, all of ye had been lost. Each day . . . . I transmit to the sons the honors of their fathers, and when some misfortune falls upon Egypt, ye abandon your duty. . . . . I administer justice every day, hearkening to every complaint that comes to me. And ye! what have ye accomplished oh, my warriors? Ye have remained in your tents and in your fortified camps, and ye gave no counsel to my army. I recommended to each of ye at his post, to take note of the day and the hour of the battle, and behold, one and all, ye have done ill; not one of you arose to aid me with his hand. . . . . I govern Egypt like my father, the Sun, and there was not found one to take heed . . . and to forewarn the land of Egypt. While, on this fortunate day, sacrifices are offered up in Thebais, in the city of Ammon, great is the fault committed by my soldiers and my horsemen. It is greater than can be told, for if I have made manifest my valor neither the archers nor the horsemen came with me. The whole world has made way to the efforts of my arm; and I was alone, and no other one was with me. That is what, of truth, I have done in the sight of my army."

When the archers and the horsemen came in, one after the other, from their camps toward the evening hour, they found the whole region in which they were marching covered with dead bodies bathed in their blood—all good warriors of Kheta, valorous champions of their prince. When daylight illuminated the land of Atesh, the foot could not find place, so numerous were the dead. Then, the army went up to glorify the names of the king:

"Good and mighty man of war, with the heart that cannot be shaken, thou dost the work of thine archers and of thy mounted men! Son of the god Toum, fashioned from his own substance, thou hast wiped out the land of Kheta with thy victorious falchion! It is thou, oh good warrior! who art the lord of armies. There is no king like to thee who does battle for his soldiers on the day of conflict. It is thou, oh king of the great heart! who art the foremost in the strife; it is thou who art the greatest of the brave, before thine army, and in the presence of the whole world risen up against thee. It is thou who dost reign over Egypt and chastise the barbarian races. . . . . The loins of the land of Kheta are thine forever."

IX.

"However, on the next day, so soon as it was daylight on the Earth, Rameses caused the battle to be joined afresh, and rushed into the combat like a bull that dashes among the geese. . . . . The warriors, in their turn, went into the fight like the hawk darting upon his prey. . . . . And the king hurled flames into the faces of his foes, like the Sun, when he appears in the morning, darting his fires on the wicked. . . . . The great lion that walked beside his coursers, fought with him; rage filled all his members, and whoever approached him was overthrown. The king seized upon them or slew them, so that not one could escape. Hewn to pieces in front of his horses, their dead bodies, extended on the ground, formed but a single heap of bleeding remains."*

One circumstance which has frequently repeated itself in scenes of warfare, rendered the disaster

---

* See the Vicomte de Rougé at the passage cited.

that befell the army of the confederates still more decisive. With a river close behind them, they seem to have had for their line of retreat nothing but the bridge leading to the city which they had wished to defend. Toward it the main struggle concentrated; Mei-Amoun, guided by his terrible military instinct, doing his utmost to force his way as far as that bridge, and Khetasar, his antagonist, fighting desperately to cover its approaches.

[There, the forests of spears, the clouds of arrows, the shields and the chariots crossed and re-crossed each other, and met in the deadly shock of battle with such re-echoing uproar that the Earth trembled to its depths, as though Apophis, the great serpent, had broken away from the chains with which the gods have fastened him to the foundations of the world.*

There valiantly fought, and not ingloriously fell, around the chief commander of the Khetas, his most faithful warriors, such as Grabatusa his squire, and Khirapsar, his librarian or *rhapsodist*;†

---

* In the Egyptian mythology, Apophis, the serpent, is the great enemy of the Sun; in several hypogees he is represented as struggling against the gods of the Amenti, who succeed in capturing and chaining him. See Champollion's *Letters from Egypt*.

† *Writer of Books*, says the text.

The City of Atesh (according to Wilkinson and the Paintings at Ipsamboul.)

and his most tried lieutenants, such as Rabsuna, chief of the archers, and Tarekennas, general of the cavalry. But, when Rameses the II. had hewn a broad and bloody passage for himself to the banks of the river over the bodies of these champions of Asia, mangled and yet palpitating beneath the wheels of his chariot, the defeat of the confederated army, now cleft in twain and without any common rallying-point, degenerated into a frightful rout, in which death in every form struck down the fugitives. Thousands of men fell under the sword, some to rise no more and others to survive themselves, mutilated as they were for life, by the terrible hooked chariot-scythe. And if the river spared a few who, following Masraim, the brother of their king, succeeded in swimming across, it swallowed up a far greater number and, especially noted among them, "the chieftain of the land of Tonira, and the prince of the bad race of the Khirabs, who was *separated from his warriors while flying before king in the direction of the water.*"

From the foot of the walls to which he had been pushed back step by step, all the time fighting, Khetasar, beholding the tremendous disaster that his gallantry had been unable to avert, resolutely took the only course that presented itself to him to save his capital from the consequences of an assault that had now become unavoidable.]

He turned with his hands extended toward the smiling sun. . . . .

He sent forth to invoke the great name of his Majesty: "It is thou who art the Sun, the god of the two horizons! It is thou who art *Soutekh*, the great conqueror, the son of heaven; Baal is in all thy members. Terror is in the land of Kheta, in such wise that thy feet are on her reins forever."

Announcement was made that a messenger had presented himself bearing a writing addressed to the great names of Majesty. . . . May this writing satisfy the heart of the god Sun, the mighty Bull, loving justice; the supreme King who himself directs his soldiers; the sword of terror; the rampart of his army on the day of battle: the King of Upper and of Lower Egypt, with the mighty courage and the boundless ardor; the Sun, lord of justice, the chosen one of the god Phra, the son of the Sun. . . . . Rameses Mei-Amoun.*

The slave says, addressing his Majesty: "My good master, son of the Sun, since Ammon has taken thee from out his loins and has given thee all the countries united together, that Egypt and the

---

* This series of titles constitutes the official protocol of King Rameses II.

people of Kheta may be slaves beneath thy feet; Phra has granted to thee, dominion over them. Thou canst slaughter thy slaves; they are in thy power; not one of them will contend against thee. Thou camest yesterday, and thou hast slain an infinite number of them; thou comest to-day,—do not continue the slaughter. . . . We are prostrate on the ground, ready to obey thy orders: oh valiant king! honor to the race of warriors! grant to us the breath of life." . . . .

Then his Majesty caused the chief leaders of the army to come, and gathered them together that they might hear the message of the great Prince of Kheta . . . . so as to write an answer. They said to his Majesty: " He hath done well, he throws his heart before the supreme king, his lord; he makes no conditions. . . . He does homage to thee to appease thy wrath."

[The king hearkened to their word and gave the vanquished his assurance of pardon and clemency; then, addressing himself to the Œris assembled in a throng around him, he added:

" Give yourselves up to rejoicing, oh my comrades; let it ascend to heaven!

" We have triumphed over the strangers by our might; we have fallen upon them like lions and we have pursued them like hawks. We have crossed their rivers, burned their fortified places, annihilated their guilty souls. The terror of my name has hovered over them and their hearts have been filled with it.

"Rejoice, then, oh my warriors!

"I am for the land of Kemi what the God Month has been. I have done battle with all the parts of the earth. Ammon-Ra has been at my right and at my left (in the battles;) his mind has inspired my own and has prepared the downfall of my enemies. Ammon-Ra, my father, has brought the whole world low beneath my feet, and I am on the throne forever."]

Thereupon, Rameses, directing his march southward, returned peaceably to Egypt with his princes and his army, leaving all the nation terrified at his exploits, and the princes prostrating themselves before him, doing homage to his countenance.

"His Majesty arrived in the city of Rameses Mei-Amoun,* the *great image of Phra*, and rested between his royal double pylons with a serene existence, like the Sun in his double abode in the heavens."

---

* Erected by the Asiatic captives and the Hebrews between the present sites of Heliopolis and Suez on the fresh water canal which once ran, and, after an interval of 3000 years, is again to run from the Nile to the Red Sea.

X.

WHEN, some time after that period, Rameses led back his army to his country, laden with the spoils of the East, and dragging numberless captives in its train; when, having passed through the cities of the Delta and the Heptanomis, more as a divinity than as a simple mortal, he came to the great temple of Thebes, to make in the presence of all Egypt, the emphatic recital of which we have just given the substance; and then, in enumerating, in grand outlines, the palpable results of his conquests; the roving tribes of the North hurled back and restrained within their native steppes, by the sword or by the faith of treaties; the frontiers of the Empire pushed beyond the Taurus and the Tigris and covered by military colonies which, from the Euxine to the Ocean, guaranteed the fidelity of nations that were vassals or in tutelage,—he terminated, at last, with "the tributes imposed, their weight in gold and silver; the number of weapons and horses; the quantities of ivory and of incense for the temples; the grain and other products which each subjugated country was to furnish, and the aggregate of which equalled all the imposts that the arms of the Parthians or Roman power have raised since then!"*—Assuredly, it was a fine day in the life of that man and of his people, whatever may have been the price that one and the other had paid for it!

No doubt that in the thinned ranks of the victors many a vacant place summoned the tears of many a family, for fathers, sons and husbands who had remained on the roads they had traversed. If we are to believe testimony quite unanimous,† Rameses himself, as he first re-appeared upon his natal soil, but narrowly escaped the plottings of a brother armed against his life, and had to inflict condign punishment upon his own flesh and blood. But the broodings of domestic misfortune and private sorrow were lost in the intoxication of triumph and the glory shared by all; for it is the peculiar quality of great events to draw closer the bonds of fellowship that unite communities, in rejoicing as in grief, and to cause generations to sympathize with one another athwart the lapse of time.

More than three thousand years have gone since these events, and yet we, who know how much each of its tardy steps of progress cost humanity; we who have it in our power to connect with the labors of Rameses and of his companions their ultimate

---

* Tacitus: Annals, Book II. ch. 60 and 61.
† Herodotus, Diodorus, Manetho.

results, which in their time no one could even conjecture beforehand,—with their complete victories over the roving tribes, the whole future of the western world based upon agriculture and the rearing of permanent cities;—with their gigantic journeyings, the enlargement of general views with regard to the world, and the drawing nearer together of a part of the long dispersed fragments of human tradition;—well, we confess aloud that, far from being tempted to smile at the ingenuous emphasis with which these men of the antique time express themselves and their infatuated delight in the indulgence of their own pride, we cannot remain coldly unsympathetic with the invocation of the day that we have mentioned, however deeply hidden it may be in the strata of history; and we feel irresistibly drawn to applaud the words of the high priest of Thebes responding to Mei-Amoun in the name of his God:

["May thy return be joyous!

"Thou hast pursued, and dispersed the barbarians; thou hast broken their bows and triumphed over their leaders. The world has seen thee, at my command, pierce the heart of the accursed nations, and make free the breath of those who followed thee under my sacred ensigns; and the world has stood still before thee! . . . My mouth doth praise thee!"]

"Thus," says the bard Penta-ur, in conclusion, "Thus Rameses, child of the Sun, and friend of Ammon, seated himself upon his throne, like the Sun, forever, all the nations of the Earth having been subdued by him."

At this point historical truth is found to disagree with the lyrical enthusiasm of the poet, for, although the achievement of Rameses, the battle of Atesh and the occupation of that city terminated the campaign, they did not put an end to the war.

Numerous monuments offer us the pictures of many other expeditions by Rameses, and long additional lists of tribes brought under subjection by his arms. In his campaign of the year XI., he returned to attack and capture by storm several fortresses in the land of Canaan, and among them, Ascalon, which had again fallen into the hands of the rebels. It is in this locality (Askaluna) a frontier town, and not at Pelusium, that we should be tempted to place the scene of the treason of which Herodotus has left us the legendary recital. In fine, it is only in the twenty-first year of his reign that Rameses, amid the pageantries of a panegyric celebrated at Thebes in honor of Ammon, sees a solemn embassy come in from the Prince of the Khetas, soliciting a definitive treaty of peace from the Pharaoh. Khetasar then acknowledged himself the vassal and tributary of Rameses, and bound himself to furnish an auxiliary contingent whenever required. This treaty, put under the protection of the national gods of each contracting party, was carved upon a memorial pillar, and exhibited to the gaze of all, in the temple of Ammon. Reciprocal matrimonial alliances cemented it, and Rameses admitted the eldest daughter of Khetasar to his harem with the rank of one his wives.

"This peace bore lasting and prolific fruit for Egypt, where, for a very long time, engraved inscriptions recalled the fact that the tribes of Kheta and of the borders of the Nile, a thing unheard of until then,* had but one heart to serve Rameses Mei-Amoun."

---

* See the Vicomte Em. de Rougé's previously cited Memoir.

THE MONUMENTS OF RAMESES THE GREAT.

The Testimony of Herodotus, of Diodorus, and of the Bible.—Memphis and Thebes.—the Great Days of Royalty.—An Artesian Well in the time of Rameses.—The Land of Cush.—The Spears of Ipsamboul.—The old Age of Rameses.—Skeletons of Oxen and Skeletons of Kings.—Darius and the Statue of Rameses.

I.

ALTHOUGH some allowance must be made for the official hyperboles of *the great bard Penta-ur, the friend of the master of the world,* it remains a confirmed fact in history that the world had never until then beheld power so vast as that possessed by Rameses on his triumphal return from his great expedition, and that for many generations afterward it was not to witness such another.

None of Mei-Amoun's successors attained the distant boundaries that he had set to his dominion, and none of them impressed upon the soil of Egypt itself such deeply marked or such multiplied traces of their passage.

In reference to this subject, Diodorus relates that " on returning from his conquests, Sesostris re-entered the regions subject to his sway with unaccustomed pomp, bringing in his train a numberless throng of captives, along with immense booty of priceless value, a share of which he pressed upon all the temples of Egypt. That country was also indebted to him for the importation of many useful inventions.

"Having given up war, he furloughed his army, compensating its services the while, with donations of land; but his passion for renown allowing him no rest, he devoted himself to numerous and magnificent undertakings, intended at once to glorify his own name, and to defend, embellish and fertilize the soil of his country. First, he caused to be built in each city a temple in honor of the patron deity of the place. In many a locality he had causeways and embankments constructed to shield the dwellings from the annual inundation; and, in many others, he dug canals, one of which was intended to open communication between Memphis and the Red Sea.

. . . . "In order to check the incursions of the predatory Arabs, he moreover enclosed the Isthmus from Pelusium to *On* (or Heliopolis) with a wall of one thousand five hundred stadii in extent. In the temple of the god worshipped at Thebes, he consecrated a vessel of cedar wood two hundred and eighty cubits long, and plated it with gold on the outside and with silver within. He had two obelisks of very hard stone erected in front of the same temple, and thereon caused to be engraved the exact tabular statistics of his armies, his revenues, the nations that he had vanquished and the tribute that he had derived from them. Within the precincts of the temple of Hephæstus,* at Memphis, he placed his own statue and that of his wife, each thirty cubits in height and hewn from one solid block. The most difficult of all these works were executed by the captives whom he had brought from foreign regions, and he took care that the lapidary inscriptions should remind the reader that *no Egyptian had a hand in them.*"†

II.

These details, borrowed from many sources, no doubt, by the historian of Stagyra, agree with those

---

* The Greek form of the Egyptian Phtah.
† Diodorus, Book I., chap. lvi. and lvii.

that Herodotus collected four centuries earlier from the lips of the priests at Memphis, Thebes and Heliopolis, *those of the latter city being considered the best informed of all in the history of their country.**

Of the numerous monuments of Rameses II. some, such as the Isthmus wall, and the fortified cities which he had built by the tribes of Beni-Heber upon that frontier, have been swept away by the breath of thirty-three centuries, or, like the terraces which formed the artificial soil of the ancient cities along the Nile, have been covered by the miry deposits which the inundations annually heap up; others, like the canal uniting the *Seaweed Lake*, since then rediscovered in the days of our fathers,† by the very man who was for them what Rameses had been for his contemporaries, have left vestiges which science interrogates, sometimes with profit and always with interest; still others, yet standing upon the desolate banks of the river that mirrored their pristine splendor, make the modern

---

* Herodotus, Euterpe, c. III.

† On the 30th of December, 1798, the general in-chief of the Army of the East, passing from Cairo to Suez, several times crossed the vestiges of the old canal with his escort of learned men.—Napoleon, in his Memoirs dictated at St. Helena.—Description of Egypt.— J. M. Lepère, in his *Mémoire* on the communication of the Indian Ocean with the Mediterranean.

solitudes participate in the majesty of the ancient days; and finally others again, borne away to the museums and public places of the great Western capitals, are perpetual sources of study and meditation for thinking minds.

It was above all in the two great capitals of his empire, in Memphis and in Thebes, that the monumental splendor of Rameses struck the observers of antiquity.

III.*

The first of these cities, much more exposed than its rival, to the inroads of time and the invader, alike by its geographical situation and the material of which it was built, sleeps to-day, completely buried beneath the slime of the inundations and the sands of the desert. A few vague undulations of the soil alone disturbing this double shroud, have served to indicate the site of monuments the ruins of which were still, six hundred years ago, according to the statement of one of the most judicious sons of Islam, a subject of admiration and astonishment for the observer.

"Notwithstanding the immense extent of Memphis and its high antiquity," writes the Arab Abdallatif in the 13th century of our Era, "notwithstanding the vicissitudes of the various governments to whose yoke it has submitted; whatever the attempts that different peoples have made to annihilate it, to cause even its faintest vestiges to disappear and wipe out the slightest traces of its existence by transporting to other points the stones and other materials of which it was constructed; by devastating its edifices and mutilating the statues that adorned them; in fine, despite all that the ages have superadded to so many causes of destruction, its ruins still present to those who contemplate them a combination of wonders that confounds the intelligence and which the most eloquent tongue or pen might vainly attempt to describe.—The more one considers it the more one feels the admiration that it inspires augment; and every succeeding glance that one casts at its ruins is a new source of enchantment."*

Memphis was especially proud of the grand temple of its eponymic divinity Phtah,† whom the relations of Rameses with Upper Asia, whence the wor-

---

* Abdallatif translated into French by M. de Sacy.

† *Ph-t ah*=*ahi, agny.* The most ancient divinity of Vedic days. The northern origin of fire-worship seems to us indisputable.

ship of this god had descended, had taught him to honor with especial devotion. Around this temple, where all the gods of the eighteenth dynasty seem to have been concentrated, Mei-Amoun had caused to be reared, in majestic colonnades, immense blocks of white calcareous stone in order to extract which from the quarrries of Mokattan and transport them to the other side of the Nile, thousands of captives had exhausted themselves for weary years.

Moreover, in testimony of his gratitude and his piety, he had caused the monolithic statues of his wife, his children and himself, to be placed before the pylons of the sanctuary, in the attitude of religious contemplation. Well! in these palaces or temples, divinities and worshippers are plunged in the same sleep and at this day abandon to the winds of the desert the same dust; and a fallen column cast to a distance from its pedestal, including which it must formerly have measured nearly forty-five feet in height, still surmounts with all the thickness of its mutilated fragments the general level of the plain—last relic of the palmy days of Memphis!

By his warlike insignia, by the delicacy of his features, by the name of Rameses engraved upon the ornaments on his breast and on the buckle of his belt, it is impossible to mistake in him the image of the conqueror, the same one of whom Diodorus and Herodotus wrote, and whom Abdallatif admired.

IV.

One hundred and fifty leagues of navigation, ascending the windings of the Nile, over the richest soil and the most densely inhabited territory on record in all time, along a double line of towns and cities led from the city of Phtah to that of Ammon.

In latitude 25° 34', the Nile, which, after entering Egypt, directs its course between the north and the northwest, suddenly doubles on itself and runs for many scores of miles toward the east-northeast, as though it would break its way through toward the nearest sea. In this space, the valley of the river, scooped out in a wide oval like an immense amphitheatre between its two parallel chains, presents one of those sites which seem predestined by nature to receive great communities of men.

This is the point at which the lines of traffic from Africa and Arabia, of the more direct routes of the Soudan by the Oases, and of the Habesh by the Nubian tablelands, converge; it is the debouching centre of the wadys that lead to the Red Sea, and which formerly guided the way to the mines of gold, copper and emeralds in the land of the Trog-

Pylons and Portico of a Great Temple (restored according to the Egyptian Commission).

lodytes: it was there that "*No-Ammon was seated between the canals, having for ramparts the waters of waters.*"

"There this instructress of the nations rested in her strength upon Ethiopia as also upon Egypt, and had the sons of Libya and those of Phut the boundless for her champions."*

There her scattered members lie to-day.

V.

WHEN, coming up from the North, the traveller has reached the projecting angle of the Libyan range which crosses the Theban plain upon that side, he suddenly beholds unrolled before him one of the grandest spectacles that man can gaze upon here below.

A mingled surface of earth and sand nearly as spacious as the modern area of Paris, traversed by a river the width of which at its period of lowest ebb is thrice that of the Seine at St. Cloud, and rolls along its broad undulations beneath a blazing sky, its stream studded with the shafts of columns, blocks of granite and broken scraps of walls whose

---

* The prophet Nahum, ch. iii., verses 8 and 9.

fallen fragments have formed hillocks there, mutilated colossi, sphinxes and gigantic rams nearly all headless now—emblems of the Kings and gods of ancient times!

Four enormous massive groups, standing with broad spaces between them, sentinelled upon this field of ruins and holding, as though in a fasces, all these rudimentary or ornamental types of Egyptian architecture, seem to have been, at different epochs, the centres of the antique metropolis. According to the names of the wretched modern hamlets which seek shelter in their shadow, Gournah and Medinet Abou are the towns to the west of the river, going from the north, and Karnak and Luxor are those to the eastward. The first of these groups contains the commemorative monuments erected to Rameses I. by Seti and to the latter by his glorious son; the second, which exhibits traces that go back to Thothmes III., was rebuilt on a gigantic plan by Rameses-Hickpun (*haq-an*) and was the residence of the Pharaohs of the twentieth dynasty.

The principal edifices of Luxor founded by Horus (*Horemheb*) were finished by Mei-Amoun to whom, for instance, are due the two grand pylons that look out upon the Nile, as also the two obelisks mentioned by Diodorus, the smallest of which

View of Thebes (restored) during the Inundation.

now adorns the principal open square in Paris. In fine, the structures of Karnak, which contained among them the first temple of the Egyptian Empire, the revered sanctuary of Ammon-Ra, date from the time of the kings who expelled the Hycsos. They have retained the stamp of their most renowned successors, and, above all, the majestic mark of Seti and of Mei-Amoun.

To these general elements of the plan of Thebes must be added the indescribable levellings of nameless temples and palaces; the canals filled up; the granite quays undermined by the Nile, or crumbling into the sand, and the three avenues of sphinxes terminating in the pylons of Karnak, and one of which is no less than half a league in length. Then, if the reader will picture to himself the soil of a long series of artificial terraces between Gournah and Medinet-Abou,—between the river and the mountain,—which, in our days, are flooded by each overflow, where thousands of broken shafts of colonnades, splinters of capitals and fragments of monoliths, and, finally, the two colossi once so celebrated under the name of Memnon, mark the site of the temple palace of Amenoph III., and of that Rameseum which seems to have been the favorite abode of Mei-Amoun. If, moreover, on the western side, one adds to this sad picture, as a framework worthy of it, the precipitous walls of the Libyan chain, pierced like the sides of an immense vessel with galleries on galleries where sleep the generations who succeeded each other in No-Ammon for two thousand years, one will, even then, have but a very imperfect idea of the mighty remains of that city, as they are seen from the top of the slope where the sight of them drew long continued plaudits of surprise and admiration from the French Army of the East.

VI.

"Thebes," says one who was present in that array, in the monumental folio in which they have recorded their impressions, "Thebes, the foremost city of the world in the time of Homer, is still, at the present day, the most surprising. One feels as though he were in a dream while contemplating the immensity of its ruins, the vastness and majesty of its edifices, and the numberless remains of its ancient magnificence."*

In order to move, to this degree, men whom unparalleled struggles, the loved study of antiquity, and the recent conquest of Italy had saturated with

---

* Rosière's Description of Egypt.—Ancient Thebes.

The Colossi of Amenoph III, otherwise called the Statues of Memnon (restored).

the perception of the grand and beautiful, what must not Thebes have been when life animated that vast body and harmonized all its parts in one imposing whole?

What must not Thebes have been at the period when, sharing in the plenitude of glory and power attained by its chiefs, this city beheld triumphant predatory expeditions and caravans of traders streaming in from all points of the horizon, and pouring the wealth of nations into her lap? in the time when the black native of eastern Soudan and the representative of the vanquished hordes of western Asia; the Hymiarite come from the land of incense and the tattooed Pelasgian from the borders of the Hellespont; the opulent merchant of the Phœnician coasts; the pearl-fisher of the Erythrean seas; the Rotenu son of Asshur with the long trailing robe, and the humble Ben-Eber of the plains of Goshen, met annually at the foot of Mei-Amoun's throne to lay the tribute of their clans and country there? What must not Thebes have been when her temple-palaces, built and embellished by twelve generations of kings, rivalled each other in splendor and display; had for enclosures fresh thickets of palms and mimosas; bedecked themselves with parterres skilfully designed, and mirrored in the blue waters of spacious basins of marble or porphyry, the pure and severely simple lines of their architecture; when, amid floods of light under the rays of an unrivalled sun, there sparkled to the gaze the vividly colored bas-reliefs of the granite pylons, the inscriptions on rose-tinted obelisks, the giant heads of sphinxes and colossi, and when each Egyptian could contemplate in the one the grand pages of his country's past history and in the other revere the well known features of his ancestors and of the gods and heroes of his race? No voice, to-day, could tell it all, no pencil accurately retrace it, and even thought, plunging through the heaped-up dust of ages, could but catch a glimpse of its vague and feeble image.

VII.

Moreover, in order not to be drawn into grave error in the appreciation of that image, one must divest himself of all preconceived ideas based upon the plan of any modern capital. We must not forget that the dead level which now gauges society, depresses their salient heights and elevates their lower strata, was neither foreseen nor even dreamed of in the days of Theban grandeur; and that from

Bird's Eye View of a Temple-Palace at Thebes (restored according to the monuments).

this absolute ignorance of the virtual conditions of a future far beyond the ken of that period, arose the very sanction of the social inequalities which existed with that of all the forms with which the sombre logic of the human mind invested them in the material as well as in the moral order.

The dwellings of men were, then, subjected to the same law that proclaimed the monarch *son of the gods*, and made the priesthood their inspired interpreters. Around consecrated edifices built of imperishable materials, cemented with the blood and sweat of whole generations of slaves, were grouped, in accordance with this law and at intervals of greater or less space marked out by cultivated fields, the luxurious yet neither very grand nor very lasting structures of the principal functionaries of the empire,—the brick-built workshops and stores of the merchant,—the cabin of the fellah made of clay and reeds, and the mud hovel where the sable captive - - sometimes the copper-colored or white one, as well, crouching on the dungheaps of the animals entrusted to his care, dressed the bleeding cuts which the stick of his master had inflicted upon his naked body, and then sought in sleep a vision of his native land and his weeping family.

Naga and Meroe, Babylon and Nineveh, the

primitive cities in the basin of the Oxus, the Indus and the Ganges; at a later period, the cities of the Etruscans, in the West; much later still, those which the Toltecs and Aymaras built upon the table-lands of the Andes, and the emigrants from India in the forests of Hindostan; all the metropolitan marks, in fine, which men erected during their passage from the second to the third social epoch, were constructed upon this principle.

VIII.

In the time of Diodorus, the historical sense of this grand Egyptian period had already been lost to the Greeks, if, indeed, the latter had ever possessed it. The historian of Stagira has left us a description of a monument in the metropolis of the Pharaohs, which had remained an indecipherable enigma until the day when Champollion proved the identity of that monument with the Rameseum on the left bank of the Thebes.

"At the distance of ten stadii from the first tombs, where, according to tradition, the Queens of Thebes are buried, there stood," says Diodorus. "the tomb of Osymandyas. At its entrance rose a pylon in marbled stone · its breadth was two ple-

Dwelling of an Egyptian of high rank (according to mural paintings).

brae and its height forty-five cubits. After having passed it, one entered a square peristyle, each side of which measured four plethræ. It was not sustained by columns, but by animals carved in solid blocks of stone sixteen cubits in height, and carved in the ancient style. The entire ceiling, consisting of a single stone, was studded with golden stars upon a field of azure. At the end of this peristyle there was a second entrance and a pylon like the former one, but adorned with variegated carvings of perfect workmanship. Beside this second portico were three statues, each chiselled from a single block of the hard and tinted stone of Syene. One, representing a personage in a sitting posture, was the largest of all the statues in Egypt. The two others, placed near his knees, one on the right and the other on the left, were those of the mother and the daughter, and did not approach the first in size. This piece was not only remarkable for its dimensions, but it was worthy of admiration in regard to its artistic execution and the nature of the stone, which, notwithstanding its vastness, did not reveal a single crack or blemish. Upon it could be read the following inscription : *I am Osymandyas, King of the Kings ; if any should wish to know who I am and where I repose, let him surpass one of my works.* There was, also, another monolithic statue representing the mother of this king separately. It was twenty cubits in height, with three diadems on its head to indicate that the personage commemorated had been the daughter, wife and mother of kings. After the second pylon was discovered another peristyle more remarkable than the first. It was adorned with different sculptures, figuratively illustrating the war that this king had maintained against the revolted Bactrians. He had marched against them at the head of four hundred thousand foot and twenty thousand horsemen, after having divided his army into four bodies, commanded by the princes, his sons.

"Upon the first wall of this peristyle Osymandyas was represented besieging a fortress surrounded by a river, exposing himself to the blows of his enemies, and accompanied by a terrible lion which served him as an auxiliary in his combats. Among those who explain these carvings, some say that it was a real lion, tamed, fed by the king's own hand, and taught to accompany him while attacking and pursuing his enemies. Others maintain that this king, who was distinguished above all the rest for his valor and his strength, intended to sound his own praises by symbolizing his qualities in the figure of a lion. . . . Finally, at the extremity of the monument, there was, in the midst of a series of

The Ramesseum.—Hall of the Colossus.

apartments, the second library designated by the inscription: *The office of the soul.*"

Volney had declared, as early as the beginning of the present century, with the intuition of genius, that all these details too clearly pointed to Sesostris to admit of any one seeing in the name given by the Greek historian anything but the epithetic title of that monarch. Twenty years later, Champollion, applying the description of Diodorus to the ruins of the Ramescum, put together from its fragments, shattered as they may be, the pretended tomb of the Osymandyas. Excepting in dimensions, exaggerated as ever by classic antiquity, he rediscovered every particular: the double pylons; the court of the colossus; the enormous fragments of the latter, which formerly must have measured thirteen yards in height; the hall of the caryatides; the galleries, the colonnades giving access to the interior apartments, and even the library with its ultramarine blue vault studded with golden stars, and decorated with an astronomical picture. Moreover, he was enabled to detect in the mural paintings, a majestic concordance with the poem of Penta-ur, and to decipher in several legends dedicated to the great deity Ammon-Ra, these characteristic words "the habitation of Rameses Mei-Amoun in the Oph of Thebes."*

IX.

To the distant expeditions of her warriors, to her communications, more or less compulsory, with the other groups of the human race, Egypt was indebted for not only an accumulation of power and wealth, but for a more active impetus given her toward the arts, trade and industry. M. de Rougé, whose authority we cannot too frequently invoke in this place, has shown that a great intellectual development, a sort of literary cycle, had been, as it were, the natural consequence of the glory of the arms and the extension of the power of Egypt over the world. Neither the poem nor the personality of Penta-ar is an isolated phenomenon of this epoch. Papyri exhumed from the tombs contain numerous and remarkable fragments of that

---

* The restored sketches published by the great Egyptian Commission puts it in our power to offer our readers different views of this monument, the finest, perhaps, of which Thebes was so proud at the period of her greatness, and one of the most dilapidated that her enclosure of ruins now contains.

Rameseum.—Hall of the Caryatides.

literature which was in a flourishing condition at the court of the Pharaohs more than fifteen hundred years before our era. They have even preserved for us the names of the Egyptian authors who lived in the vicinity of Rameses, or of his immediate successors, and whose theological, philosophical historical, romantic or poetical compositions propagated and multiplied by the bureaux of calligraphy, or, in other words, copying offices, of the period, were not without their echoes among their contemporaries, nor without influence upon the general current of the human mind. This rising movement of intelligence upon the borders of the Nile seems to correspond in time with those achievements of a similar nature that, on the banks of the Indus and the upper Ganges, distinguished the heroic age of the Aryan tribes that used the Sanscrit tongue. From that time forth, anterior Asia also undoubtedly had her writers and her artists. But Egyptian domination ruled in this region during too long a lapse of centuries not to leave the imprint of the conquerors deeply stamped upon its manners, institutions, and religious notions. Thus, the style of the most ancient cuneiform inscriptions differs but little from that of the carved hieroglyphics and the papyri of the Egyptians. Still more, a *stele* found among the ruins of a Theban temple, a veritable *ex voto* of those remote times, exhibits to us a sovereign from beyond the Tigris, the father-in-law and vassal of a Pharaoh of the twentieth dynasty sending a solemn embassy to his son-in-law to obtain the temporary cession or the loan of an Egyptian idol of great repute in order that it might exorcise one of his daughters who was possessed of an evil spirit.

"Four centuries of intercourse in peace and war had multiplied the intimate relations between the Egyptians and the Asiatic nation. The former made journeys to Mesopotamia: these were officers sent by the prince to govern the provinces, to superintend the stations established and command the garrisons posted in the fortified places. The Asiatic came to Egypt, far as it was, either to consult the Egyptian physicians whose learning was already famous,—the wizards, probably, who contended with Moses,—or to carry on trade. The metal cups found in the ruins of Assyria are covered with Egyptian emblems, and the Kings of Tyre wore a diadem patterned after the *pschent* of the Pharaohs.

"We also discover the influence of the literary forms usual in Egypt among a people whose first steps excite a lively interest everywhere. The Bible shows us, at this epoch, the sons of Jacob, of

Slaves, under the 18th dynasty, making brick.

whom Divine protection had made a new nation, exhausting their strength in constructing in the Delta a city to which the holy book gives the name of Rameses.

"Frequently mentioned in our papyri, the place there bears the name of Rameses Mei-Amoun, and the scroll-boxes (even a statue) of the great conqueror have been found among its ruins. Rameses II., then, was the persecutor of the Israelite family whose increasing number became a subject of alarm for his policy. This king could not banish the remembrance that, upon several occasions, the wandering tribes of Asia, filling up lower Egypt by their incursions, had driven out the Pharaohs.

"It was then that Moses, having been rescued by the daughter of the sovereign, was reared in the palace and instructed in all the lore of Egypt. The concordance of the periods of time, and the minutiæ of the narrative do not leave room to attribute these wants to any other Pharaoh. Rameses is the only one who by his reign of sixty-eight years presents a sufficient lapse of time for the long withdrawal of Moses to the deserts of Arabia. The book of Exodus informs us, in fact, that the king whose anger Moses had aroused *died after a very long time*, and that then only did the prophet venture to return to Egypt. . . . .

"Moses, therefore, was reared in a country which had carried art and industry to a very high pitch, and at a moment when its literature shone with more than usual brilliance. It is easy to recognize in the Egyptian texts, the peculiar turn of verses and the parallelism of the ideas or of the expressions which form the special character of Hebrew poesy. The earliest sacred writers even have directly borrowed from the priestly annalists certain expressions whose energy and beauty have long been admired, and it is no mean glory for the poet Penta-our and for the other men of letters assembled at the court of Rameses Mei-Amoun to have had a considerable share in the literary education of the Hebrew legislator."*

X.

BEFORE going farther we should point out the fact that the cruel policy practised by Rameses toward the Hebrews, was not exclusively his own. It had been that of all his predecessors. A very curious painting found at Thebes, upon the walls of a burial chapel attributed to Thothmes III., shows

---

* Viscount E. de Rougé in the paper already cited.

Captives building a temple; from a mural painting.—18th dynasty.

us prisoners of war employed in kneading clay, moulding bricks and building the walls of a temple to Ammon under the surveillance of Egyptian superintendents or overseers armed with heavy staves. The inscription informs us that these *prisoners at hard labor*, " are captives taken by His Holiness to work upon the temple of his father Ammon." When copied by the engraver's art, does not this scene look like an illustration of the folowing passage in Exodus: ch. i. v. xiii. and xiv.

" And the Egyptians made the children of Israel to serve with rigor :"

" And they made their lives bitter with hard bondage, in mortar, and in brick, and in all manner of service in the field: all their service, wherein they made them serve, was with rigor."

History can bring to the support of the Biblical text still more formal testimony than the preceding. There are legible upon the back of a hieratic papyrus which, unfortunately, has been very much mutilated, but which may be referred to the nineteenth dynasty, these characteristic lines : " That for twelve years, these men, entrusted with the making of bricks, be kept and closely watched in the workshops, so as to see that they deliver exactly the number of bricks that they are ordered to make, *without rest or cessation !*" (A papyrus of the Anastasi Collection No. 3, page 2.)

This working-up of the captive and the slave pushed to its farthest limits, *i.e.* mutilation and death, was *the law of nations* of a historic age, which did not cease even with the most civilized countries until after the advent and triumph of Christianity : that law of nations, of which, long after the time of Rameses, the Assyrian monarchs, the Dorian Republics of Greece and the Roman patriciate, were to make many another ferocious application, and which, even while we write, still entangles, with its long-surviving roots, the eastern half of modern Europe, and all the countries yet under the yoke of the late-comers of wandering barbarism.

XI.

At Thebes, as in all the great cities of the valley of the Nile, the sacred edifices enclosed within their limits between the *pronaos* and the sanctuary of the gods, a spacious hall which, owing to the numerous columns supporting its massive ceiling of carved and tinted granite, received the title of *hypostyle* from the Greeks. The one that Seti I. caused to be built in the temple of Karnak is celebrated among

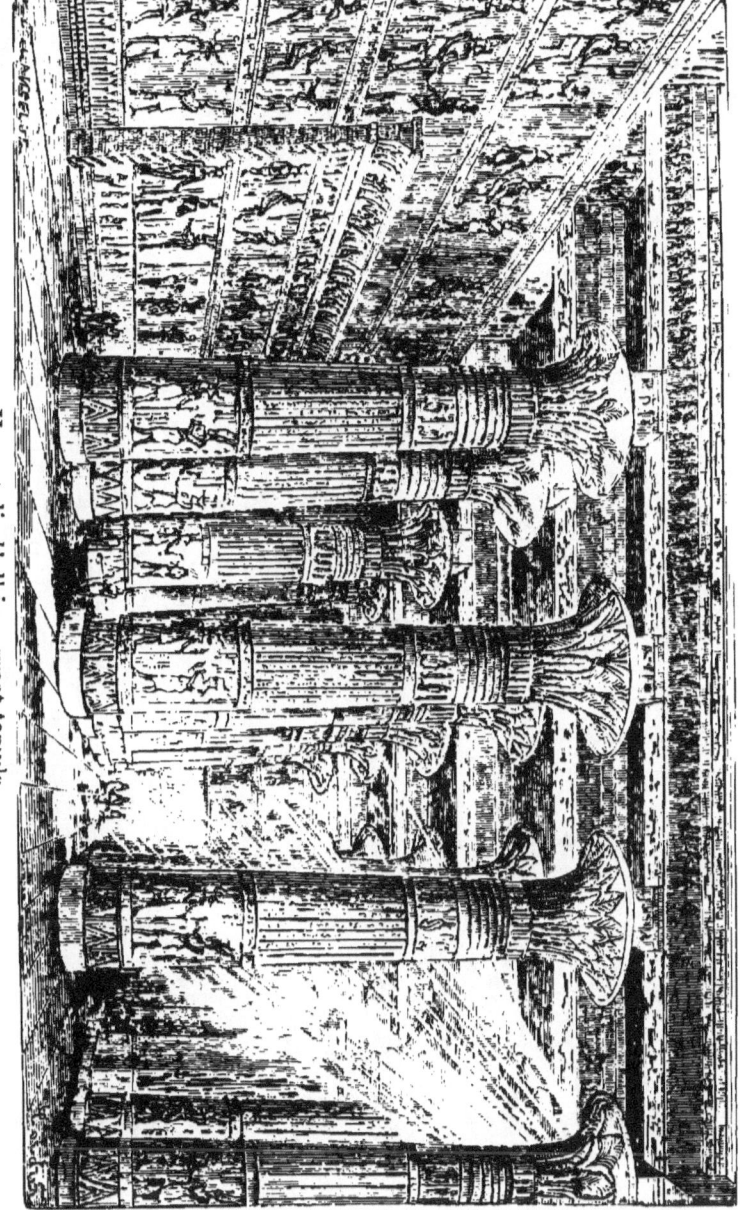

Hypostylic Hall in a great temple.

them all for its dimensions—one hundred yards by fifty—and its hundred and thirty-four columns still standing, a dozen of which sustain the central part of the ceiling, at the height of seventy feet from the soil, upon capitals of twenty yards in circumference. The dimensions of these halls, even in the absence of other indications, would bear witness to the purpose for which they were destined. In the shadow of these groves of columns, where apertures curiously cut in the upper part of the cornice or windows hewn through the solid granite allowed only a subdued heat to penetrate, and just enough light to illuminate the reliefs and the tintings of the great mural scenes, the monarch, seated on a magnificent throne, between the mementoes of his ancestors and the images of his gods, presided at the meetings of the priesthood and high dignitaries of the empire; gave audience to the ambassadors of foreign nations and to deputations from vassal nomes and provinces; adjudged, as a tribunal of last appeal, the disputes of cities or of individuals; listened to the complaints of his subjects or the outcry of their need; in.fine, held the great days of the royal sway.

The scribes, a very busily employed race of functionaries, whose learned body replenished its ranks from the colleges of the priesthood, took down, on the spot, the minutes of these sessions of absolute power. Subsequently, when the importance of the subject demanded it, the series of all the orders and of all the administrative measures thereunto appertaining was recapitulated on a monumental *stele*, destined to remind the population therein interested of the vigilance and solicitude of the prince. And, in sooth, these *stones of testimony* which have survived until our own time, are not the least instructive of the monuments that will put modern science in a condition to reconstruct the genuine history of the Egyptian period, of which, more faithfully than the others, perhaps, they represent the real aspect, the characteristic traits and the inner private life.

It is with this view that we do not feel as though we could omit from this study on Rameses and his time, a few passages from a document of this description dating from the commencement of the reign of that prince. We borrow them from the interpretations jointly agreed upon by the English orientalist Birch, and our learned compatriot M. Lenormand.

XII.

. . . . " When he had subdued the land of Ethiopia, trodden the Libyans beneath his sandals, and rooted his sceptre among them; after terror had overwhelmed Wentnowr and the Akars, the living and life-bestowing god, the representative of Seth and Ammon, the king sun, the guardian of truth approved by Phrah, the director and defender of the land of Kemi, the child of the gods, the beloved one of Ammon, Rameses, the eternal life-giver, descended at Memphis to accomplish toward the divine triad of that city ceremonies of thanksgiving.

"On the twenty-fourth day of the month *paoni*, in the third year of his reign, as he was seated on his throne of the purest gold, and, with his head adorned with two ostrich plumes emblematic of justice, was causing the names of the regions from which gold was obtained to be registered in his presence, and was giving orders that the roads leading to them and unprovided with water should be supplied with fountains, there was mentioned, among others, the country of Okan where gold abounded, but the route to which was utterly destitute of springs. His Majesty was informed of the distress of the workmen employed in the extraction and preparatory washing of the precious metal, many of whom had perished of thirst on the way with the asses they drove thither. In fine, the condition of things was such that it could not continue without leading to the abandonment of the rich placers in question.

"At this moment, the officer of the palace whose business it was to lead visitors to the foot of the throne, breaking silence, announced to Rameses that the leading personages of the Okau country were present and humbly awaiting the favor of an audience:

"Behold them, oh king, with their arms uplifted toward thy throne and drawing nigh with reverence to look upon thy sacred features, in order that they may unfold to thee the deplorable condition of their country, and beseech thy limitless power to remedy it."

And permission to speak having been accorded to the chiefs of Okau, they said:

"Thy power has no bounds; it is like the power of Mandu and of Ammon, whose depositary thou art, here below: if thou wert to give orders to the night, the light would instantly appear. We come then, in all haste, to implore thy Majesty to do something in behalf of these gold mines, since thou art he who dost shine, at present, on the throne of the world. Thou wilt not reject our prayers, thou who hast but to say to the mountain spring to leap forth, in order to behold the abyss of the waters of the heavens fly open at the sound of thy voice; for thou art the sun *made flesh*, all of whose orders are obeyed, all of whose words are made good, oh thou, our lord and our master! . . . ."

Thus spake the chiefs of Okau; then a great dignitary, the second in the empire, the viceroy of Ethiopia, came forward to sustain their request with the weight of his opinion.

"It is but too true," said the royal son of Cush. In their country the grass has been burned since the reign of the gods, and all the Pharaohs, thy predecessors, desired that a well should be dug on the borders of the road that leads thither, but their wish was in vain. At the command of Seti, of glorious memory, search was made to the depth of one hundred and twenty cubits for the sheet of water intended to refresh the soil: it did not reach the surface. But thou, if thou saidst to Hapi-Mou, thy father and the father of the gods: *Cause the water to cover the face of the desert!* it would be as it is with all thy words, all thy orders which are fulfilled in thy very presence. If they are instantly obeyed is it not because thou art dear to the gods of thy ancestors above all the monarchs that have reigned since the sun?" . . .

To the royal son of Cush, and to the chiefs of the country of Okau, Rameses replied: "Your request is just; as you have declared, there has been no well dug near this road since the reign of the gods; and, *it is my will* that a well shall be made there to yield water without ceasing, as though it sprang from the exhaustless bosom of the Nile. The gods who heap their favors upon me, and who have flooded my heart with joy, will help me in this circumstance. Under their protecting auspices, I proclaim, then, the order to pierce a living well at one of the intermediate stations of the road that leads from the Nile to Okau. Let this order, copied by the scribes on duty, be reproduced and published by the aid of the chief of the transcribing bureau, in my double dwelling of light, and let a copy of the order be sent to the royal son of my land of Cush, who continues charged with its execution."

And the prince of Nubia, *superintendent of the land of Cush*, having got together the necessary workmen recommenced the task that had been begun during the reign of Seti, and caused it to be pushed with so great activity, *that nothing like it had been done since there were kings in Egypt*. The caving in of the soil, and the infiltration of sand into the tube of the well, were checked successfully by linings of reeds woven in mats or interlaced in fascines* and with such excellent result that the viceroy was enabled to send word to Mei-Amoun that the water was spouting four cubits above the soil, but that to raise it to twelve, as his Majesty had ordered with his own lips, it was still indispensable that a skilled workman should be sent. . . . Shortly afterward the sovereign word of Rameses had its full effect: "The king of the waters has hearkened to the king of the earth, the well has been fortunately terminated, and abundant waters leap from its mouth and pass on to a distance to fertilize the surface of the desert and quench the thirst of the parched traveller." By a last decree, Rameses, the friend of Ammon, expressed the wish that this work of public utility should bear his name, and that a *stele* commemorative of these acts should be placed within the enclosure of the temple raised to Thoth Trismegistus, (celestial superintendent of Nubia for the supreme gods,) on the right bank of the Nile, opposite to the city of Pselkis. And it was there, at the mouth of the *wady* which leads from the river to the modern cantonal district of Olaki, that it has been found again in our time.

---

* We give this interpretation on our own responsibility; it seems to be indicated by M. Lenormand. As for Mr. Birch, the text seems to him to allude to aquatic birds playing among the reeds.

XIII.

The appellation of the land of Cush, which in the presence of the encroachments of the yellow or red branches of the human main stem, had receded from the southern plains of Asia as far as the upper basin of the Nile, still ran down in the days of Mei-Amoun from the unknown heights of Africa as far as the cataracts of Syene, thus covering all the territory that the Greeks have since called Ethiopia, and the moderns Sennaar and Nubia. The importance of these provinces in the monarchy of Rameses was such that the title of their viceroy or superintendent seems to have been, under several dynasties, one of the first that was conferred upon the heir presumptive of the empire, at his birth, and a long partnership in common, of interests and of glory, had so bound them to Egypt that Champollion did not fail to discover that the Pharaohs, full of confidence in the natives of Ethiopia, gave up to them all the administrative positions even to the command of the troops of the country. The learned Egyptian scholar has cited and deciphered in support of his assertion a great number of inscriptions still existing between the first and second cataract.*

---

* Champollion the younger: *Letters Written from Egypt and Nubia.*

Mei-Amoun, whose appanage this country appears to have been during the lifetime of his father Seti, seems also, judging by the monuments with which he endowed it, to have retained a peculiar affection for it, during the whole course of his long life.

In fact, from Philæ as far as Mount Barkal, more than two hundred leagues from Thebes and four hundred from the Mediterranean, there are few ruins, *steles* or subterranean temples that do not retain some relic, the scrolls or even the features of the great Rameses.

It is to the graphic arts, to pure archæology, that the labor of retracing the stages of this long advance specially appertain; but it is not departing from the limited circle of this sketch even, wherein the effort is to become inspired with the philosophy of history, to cite those of the localities the examination of which may prove profitable in pursuing the study of ancient manners and institutions.

XIV.

At Essebouah, stood a temple palace the avenue to which was formed by a double row of lions emblematic of courage ever on the alert. It terminated in two magnificent pylons supported by eight gigantic statues of Rameses. A bas-relief representing the fourteen daughters of that monarch makes one think that the monument dates from an advanced epoch of his reign and of his life. Moreover, it seems to have been thrown down in wantonness at some period of ferocious reaction or barbarian invasion, and the eight colossi overturned in the sand, remind us involuntarily of the *Titans struck by the bolts of Jove.**

In the *speos* or subterranean temple cut in the rocks at Derr by order of the conqueror, his image is seen seated at the farther end of the sanctuary between those of the three great ancestors of the Egyptian pantheon: Phtah, Ammon and Phra; and the legends on the walls show the same Rameses taking part as a divinity in the religious homage which he offers as a mortal, a priest and a god, all in one.

At Ibrim, which, under the name of Primis, was the landmark of the Roman empire at the time of its greatest extension toward the south, another speos was excavated in honor of Pharaoh and under the invocation of Toth and of Sate, the local divinities, through the pious care of *a royal son of Cush,* the same, no doubt, who is mentioned on

---

* Ampère: *Correspondence from Egypt and Nubia,* Letter IX.

View of Ibrim, at the present day.

the *stele* relative to the well of Okan. On the carved and painted walls of the subterranean temple " this same personage is represented rendering his respectful homage to Rameses, at the head of all the functionaries of his government."

Champollion has called attention to the fact that the mere presence of the wife of the Ethiopian prince who figured in this ceremony at the side of her husband and in advance of all the other functionaries marks an essential difference between the civilization of Egypt and that of *the rest of the East.** If the erudite French hierogrammatist had substituted the words *the modern Oriental world* for the expression above given, he would have kept closer to the exact truth. What we know of India at the epoch of the second Rama allows us to dispense with insisting on this point. Between the exquisite sentiment that revealed to the antique poet Valmiki the fresh and pure creation of Sita, and that which impelled Rameses to rear directly beside the most commemorative edifice of his life a sort of votive chapel to the Egyptian Venus for the use of the *Nofre-Ari, the royal spouse whom he loved,*† is there

---

* Champollion : *Letters written from Egypt and Nubia.*
† This inscription is the one on the grand front. "To make up for it, in the dedication carved upon the architrave, in the interior of the temple, at the end of the ordinary

not something like a bond of simultaneousness in time or of common origin?

It will be understood that we refer to the speos of Athor at Ipsamboul, *the grotto of purity* and of love, the details of which are full of interest and artistic charm, and where, from the gigantic front excavated in the rock to the ornaments on the pillars that support the vault of the three halls scooped out in its flanks, and even to the minutest adornments of its chiselled and frescoed walls, everything reveals, as it were, a tender and reverential association of thought between Rameses and the fair companion of his youth; everything bears the impress of a feeling of harmony and conjugal equality.*

When, in the time of our fathers,† the celebrated traveller Burckhardt discovered the façade of this monument, and measured its caryatides of thirty-six feet in height, he believed that he had come upon

---

legend of Rameses. is read this line, which discloses the tenderness of the Queen for Rameses: *His royal spouse who loves him, Nofre-Ari, the great mother, has constructed this resting place in the grotto of purity.* Ampère, at the place cited.

* Ampère in the place cited. The queen is charming. says the traveler, and one never grows weary of meeting everywhere with her likeness, which Pharaoh never grows tired of reproducing.

† In 1817. See the *Voyages de Burckhardt.* **French** translation. Vol. I.

The Speos of Athor at Ipsamboul (front façade restored).

the grandest thing that Egyptian art had created. What then was his astonishment when, on turning an angle of this rocky cliff, he found himself confronting four colossal figures of double dimensions, cut out in a second mountain, raising their fronts bound with the *pshent*, and their huge shoulders, high above the avalanche of sand which the wind of Libya continually rolls down from the top of the stony wall of which they form a part. There they seemed to be waiting, amid the silence of the desert the approach of some representative of modern civilization who should extricate them from the oblivion in which renown had let them sleep for thirty-three centuries.

XV.

SINCE Burckhardt's adventure, many other visitors have reached the spot, and the great temple of Ipsamboul has become the goal of the numerous tourists which Europe daily sends to the banks of the Nile. In the four stone giants, which have none like them in the world excepting the two colossi of Bamian that, from an unknown date in the past, have recalled to the inhabitants of the Paro-amisus the nameless features of a *king* and *queen* of the South,* have been recognized, even previous to any aid through the interpretation of the scroll cases, the pure and delicate graciousness and the majestic placidity that characterize all the portraits of Rameses Mei-Amoun. The portico of the *peos*, when cleared of the sand of ages which had obstructed it, yielded to the study and the admiration of the explorers a whole historical museum of which Rameses is the hero. Sixteen halls carved out in the flanks of the mountain by the chisels of the old Egyptian sculptors, are dedicated only to reproduce his deeds and to glorify his memory. Upon their walls he battles and triumphs as a warrior, sits enthroned and wields the sceptre as a king, and officiates as a pontiff. His statues, erect, with their arms crossed upon their breasts, supply the place of pillars to prop up the mountain; then, he sits in the sanctuary between Ammon, the supreme divinity, and Phrah, the Sun made a deity.

How long did the members of this strange trial assemble the same worshippers, receive the same incense? For two thousand years past, Ammon utters no more oracles, the Sun has ceased to be the eternal source of life even for the black Nubian, and the echoes of the Nile have forgotten even the name of Rameses. However, to this hour, when

---

* Alex. Burnes: *Journey to Samarcand.*

The Speos of Phra at Ipsamboul (façade restored).

the star of day, emerging from the horizon of Arabia, darts its morning ray athwart the narrow portico of the great speos of Ipsamboul, and surrounds the mutilated brows of the three antique idols with a fleeting halo, it still seems to the most indifferent passer-by, the coldest and most skeptical son of mocking Europe, as though some religious mystery were occurring in the recesses of the rock.* What, then, must have been the effect upon the imagination in those periods of implicit belief or credulous ignorance, of this daily phenomenon, skillfully managed by the priesthood of the speos, when immediately opposite to the latter, a considerable centre of population, culture and commerce covered the Eastern bank of the river now so desolate? It appears that at the time of the social upheaving directed by Moses, which, not long after Mei-Amoun's day, compelled the Pharaohs and their court, as in the days of the Hycsos, to seek an asylum in Nubia, that hospitable country could not offer them a retreat better calculated than this to fortify their resolution afresh. In what

---

* Ampère, place already cited. See in the works of Fontenelle what he states, on the authority of Ruffin, in reference to an opening made by the priests in the temple of Serapis, through which, at a certain moment, a ray of the sun fell upon the lips of the god.

school could the orphaned and banished heir of the sceptre of Rameses, the young *Haq-an* who, afterward, was Rameses III.,* wishing to become inspired with the soul of his great-grandfather so as to resume and consolidate his work, have drawn loftier lessons than those which exhaled for him from the subterranean temples of Ipsamboul?

XVI.

The ages and barbarism have so well respected the bas-relief pictures of the great temple, and their colors are still so fresh, that, according to the ingenuous expression of the Arabs, one would think that the workmen employed had hardly had time to wash their hands since they were completed.†

All these marvels of Egyptian art at the height of its splendor offer material for study the more precious that the most of it evidently dates back to an epoch in the life of Rameses, concerning which the historians of antiquity knew as little as they did of the monuments that are now engaging our attention.

---

* Manetho, in Josephus *contra Appionem.*—It is evident that the Cethos of this fragment is indeed Rameses III., son of Seti II., son of Menephtah, son of Rameses the Great.

† Ampère, place cited.

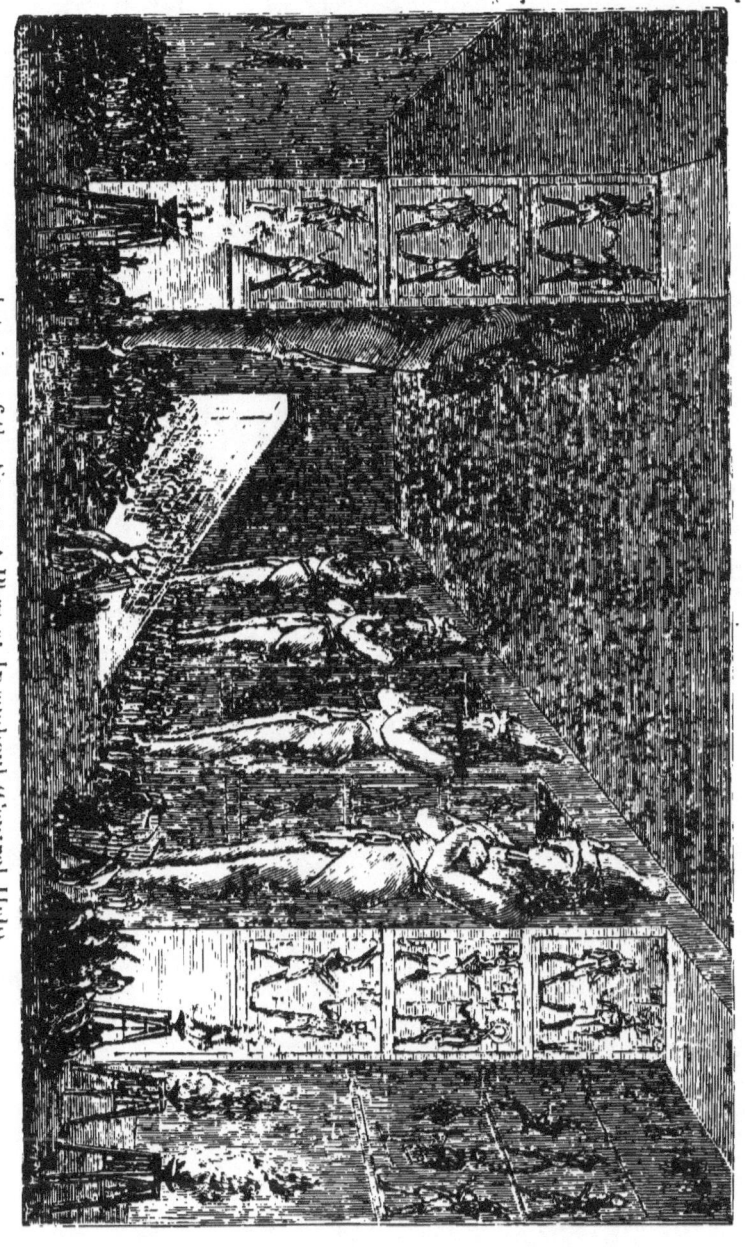

Interior of the Speos at Phra at Ipsamboul (Central Hall).

According to the legendary opinion followed by Herodotus, Diodorus and Josephus, Rameses II. from the tenth year of his reign had closed his career of battle and conquest, and the friendly fates had imposed no other care upon him than to enjoy in peace the fruit of his youthful exploits. The walls of Ipsamboul, on the contrary, along with the inscriptions that we have been enabled to put together among the ruins of the two Rameseums of Thebes, the most dilapidated of all the great king's monuments, and, also, one of the bas-reliefs of Beit-el-Wally, show him to us in his riper years, surrounded by numerous sons, and in their company fighting the same enemies against whom he had directed the expeditions of his youth, viz., the black tribes of the South and the white or yellow hordes of the North.

The picture of the grand hall of Ipsamboul, inscribed by Champollion under No. 1, offers, in this respect, along with that which the same learned antiquarian copied from the half crumbled pylon of the western Rameseum, such analogies of detail, that it is impossible to avoid considering the one a reproduction of the other. In both of them, Rameses, accompanied by three of his sons, already men grown and mounted like himself in war chariots, is pursuing, at headlong speed, a hostile army whose heavy garments covered with mantles, hair gathered up in a single lock in the middle of the cranium, and pallid complexion, would indicate their origin to be from beyond the Oxus, even did the legends of these historic pages fail to give them the name of *Khetas*. At Thebes, as at Ipsamboul, these obstinate antagonists of Rameses are seen seeking refuge in a fortified place, the walls of which four Egyptian princes, other sons of the conqueror, have just assailed. We know not whether the name of the besieged town has been discovered at Ipsamboul, only the last half of it having been preserved among the ruins of the Theban monument. But that termination is quite significant, for it reads: *apur*, and this Sanscrit ending alone indicates some locality far to the Eastward.

XVII.

It has not been allotted, so far as we know, to men who have been summoned to make themselves felt in the world on the eve of great upheavals in the social strata or in the human mind, to find repose anywhere but in the tomb. Everything, therefore, induces us to believe that, contrary to the assertions of the ancients, Rameses must have

The Speos of Ipsamboul. The cleared fronts, seen from the right bank of the Nile.

passed the long years of his reign struggling, sword in hand, to maintain outside, the eminent influence of his name and the completeness of his conquests. More than once, no doubt, he was obliged, as Charlemagne was, in long after ages, to hasten, in his grey hairs, from his Southern frontiers, still threatened, as they were, by the savage barbarism of the Nahazis, to those of the North which were still agitated by the movements of the Aryan communities pushing the Semites and the Pelasgians before them on all the routes of the West. More fortunate than the son of Pepin, was he spared the sight of the tempests that were to sweep away the dynasty that had been the labor of his life? And if his iron constitution secured him the honor so coveted by the Pharaohs, of twice celebrating the trentenary panegyric of his coronation, could he in this enjoyment of his old age carry his sceptre and his harp as high as the level of his pride? No one can tell. History and the monuments are silent on this score. The first accords to him a reign of from sixty-six to sixty-eight years, but dating from the sixty-second, the monuments preserve a mournful silence in reference to this great name.*

---

* The latest date found at Ipsambul is of the 38th year. The rocks of Silsilis mention the 40th and the 44th; the walls of the Serapeum the 55th. Finally, a *stele* in the Florence Museum is dated in the 62d.

Like the patriarchs his contemporaries, Rameses saw a numerous family born and reared around him. The monumental inscriptions have acquainted us with the names of twenty-three princes, his sons, and thirteen of his daughters, of whom five are dignified with the title of queens. One, with a name anything but full of euphony for our ears—Baunt-Ant—seems to have been the female Benjamin of his declining years.

But he also lived to see most of his children die one by one, around him, including all of his sons who had taken part in the struggles, the combats, and the triumphs of his riper age. He survived by thirteen years the man who, among all the rest, he and his subjects regarded as the most worthy to succeed him, viz., the prince Sha-em-Jom, and, at last, he had to leave his sceptre in feeble hands. Then, as the good king Priam was made to feel in later years, he had to admit that a lengthy lineage is not always a guarantee of good fortune and stability; that old age is rarely a blessing, and that those whom the gods love, die young.*

The prince Sha-em-Jom, so popular among his contemporaries, and of whom Egypt, during the troubled reign of his brother Menephtah doubly felt the loss, has left tokens of remembrance on a

---

* Homer's *Iliad*, ch. 24, and Menander's *Fragments*.

great number of monuments, particularly at Memphis, of which he was governor or viceroy. The lapidary inscriptions show him to us presiding in this character from the thirtieth year of his father's reign over the grand panegyrics which were celebrated every four years in honor of the god Phtah.

The French savant M. Mariette, to whom we are indebted for an interpretation of these inscriptions, has found a great number of others dedicated to the same prince, in the recesses of the Serapeum of Memphis, that strange necropolis peopled with statues of Apis or sacred bulls whose epitaphs have enabled that indefatigable reader of inscriptions to regulate, by genuine figures, the hypothetical dates of a quite important portion of Egyptian chronology, and to bring the undeniable testimony of these humble four-footed creatures to bear in proving or disproving the existence of royal dynasties and monarchs claiming to be the children of gods.

According to all appearances, Sha-em-Jom was buried in the Serapeum, where, after the lapse of thirty-three centuries, M. Mariette thinks that he has discovered his mummified remains. We can do no better than to transcribe in this place the exact language of the report on the subject which that celebrated expert has addressed to his European brethren:

"Three of the five Apis that died during the reign of Rameses II. were buried in chambers No. 2, 3 and 4 of the small subterranean excavations. The other two had been deposited in one hollow chamber, the wall of which bears the date of the year 55 of the great king. One died when the prince Menephtah, who at a later period was to succeed his father Rameses II., had taken the place of Sha-em-Jom in the government of Memphis, and from the position of the mummy, I do not think

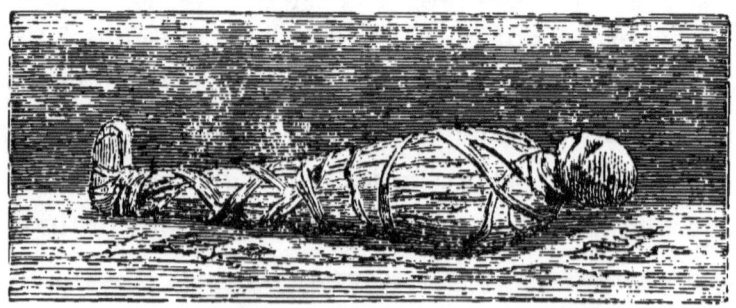

A mummy in its bandages.

that it is to this Apis that the date written on the wall refers. Consequently, the other died in the year 55, and this observation is interesting if, as may be the case, the mummy of which I have recovered the remains, instead of being that of Apis was that of prince Sha-em-Jom himself. This new point would be worth extended explanation. Let the reader imagine a mummy in the human form destroyed in all its lower parts from the breast downward. A thick mask of gold now at

Case containing a mummy.

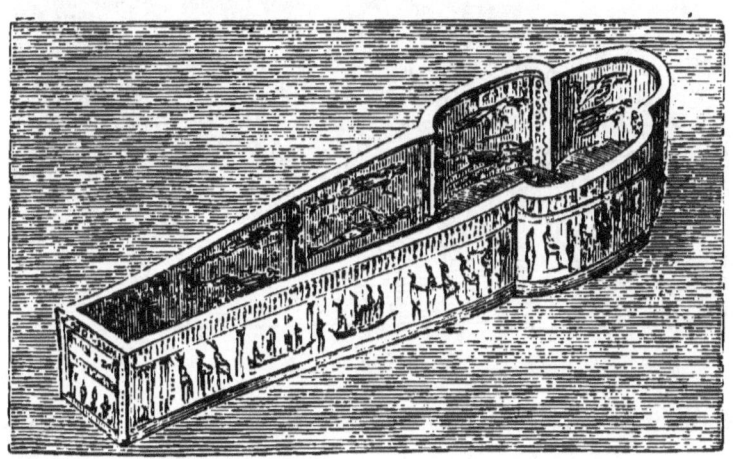
Interior coffin to contain the case.

the Louvre covered its face. Around the neck were two chains, also of gold, to one of which were suspended three amulets. As for the interior, it *presented nothing but a mass of odoriferous bitumen mingled with shapeless bones, in the midst of which were buried two or three pieces of jewelry with golden clasps containing small plates of glass.* Finally, near this singular monument, I picked up a large beetle in greyish *steatite*, a little pillar of green feldspar and a score of small funereal statues of the human form.

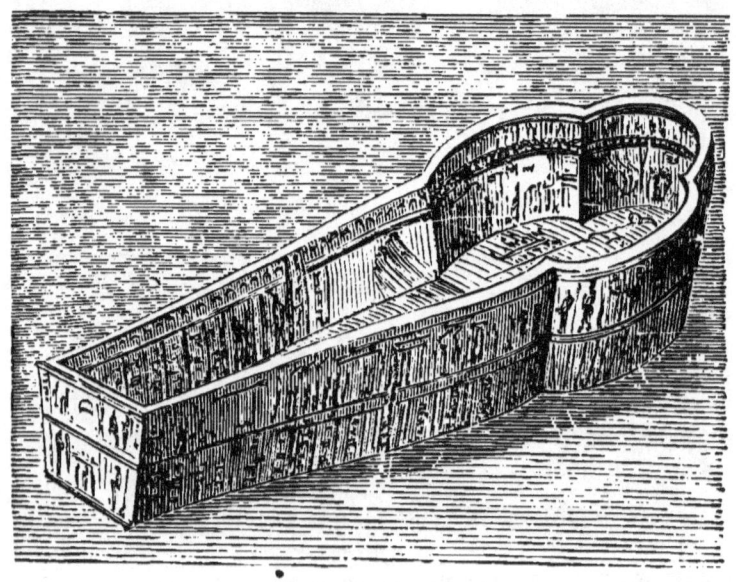

Exterior coffin.

Such was our Apis, and some estimate of the embarrassment this discovery occasioned us may be had when it is furthermore known that while all the monuments found above the mummy indicate the title and name of Sha-em-Jom only, all those on the contrary that were discovered in the neighborhood mention the name and usual qualifications of Osorapis. Is this an Apis? or is it the mummy of Sha-em-Jom, who, dying in the 55th year of his father's reign, made it a point to be buried in the finest of the tombs that adorned the cemetery of the city of which he was the governor, therein fol-

Sarcophagus.*

lowing the example of the other grandees of Egypt, who had themselves buried at Abydos near the tomb of Osiris?"

To sum up, was this funereal windfall, this decayed *magma*, the remains of the beloved son of Rameses, of the selected heir of his vast empire, or

---

* These sarcophagi in porphyry, in basalt or in alabaster, formed the fourth and last outside covering of mummies of high rank.

simply those of a bull fattened in a sacerdotal stall?
Is there not in the doubt itself, a keen satire on
renown and death, as bitter as any that history
has ever gathered in the tomb?

We have elsewhere remarked the relations that
exist between the duration of the reigns of the
Pharaohs and the splendor of their tombs. That
of Rameses should, consequently, have surpassed
all the rest in magnificence. It was the third to
the right in the valley of tombs. At the present
day nothing remains of it but a mass of shapeless
ruins. All *the funereal abodes of the holy mountain* of
the West having been violated and overturned by
the Persians at the time of the invasion of Cambyses, those barbarian conquerors wreaked their
revenge particularly on the tomb of the man in
whom was incarnated the Egyptian nationality in
its struggles against the men of the North, justly regarded by these barbarians as their ancestors.
However, long before this period of warlike vengeance, the priestly reaction which had put an end
to the dynasty of Rameses and his successors;
which had identified the patron deity of this martial family with Typhon, the genius of evil; which
had pursued the images of Sethos even to where
they were found on the scroll-box of the great king,

—had this reaction really respected his memory and his coffin!

XVIII.

Whatever may have been the causes of the revolution that wrested from the descendants of Rameses the sceptre of Egypt and transferred it to the family of the priest Peor, it cannot be considered as a reassertion of human dignity, outraged by the unbounded-haughtiness of the Pharaohs of the eighteenth, nineteenth and twentieth dynasties. A mere shifting from one set of hands to another of privileges and vices, it momentarily profited the priestly order only to the detriment of the vital forces of the nation whose decline and downfall it hastened. A people can never with impunity be taught to contemn what once they worshipped. Under the anathema which fell upon her military spirit and warlike energy, Egypt sank back upon herself like her granite sphinxes crouching near the entrance of her temples. Thenceforth, concentrating in the adoration of natural phenomena, an activity which had no other outlet, she strove to connect with the subtleties of nascent metaphysi cal science, the rude conceptions of her original mythology, and made everything else subservient to this vain toil; men and things, principles and facts, art, industry and intelligence alike. With her everything passed into the condition of a symbol, and every symbol became stone, until, petrified herself like the objects of her idolatry, she did not notice the billows of the human race that were flooding up around her.

Even then, upon that soil struck with a paralysis which lingers there still, one grand memory alone survived and covered this corpse of a nation with the name of Rameses as with a protecting ægis. One day Darius, entering Memphis as its master, penetrated to the temple of Phtah and gave orders that his own statue should be placed in front of those of the native kings, and even of the colossal figure of Rameses Mei-Amoun. But, upon hearing this order of the victorious monarch, the prophet of the temple opposed it in these terms: "Thou hast not done, oh king, all that Rameses did, since the latter not only subdued as many nations as thou, but he also conquered the Scythians whom thy Persians could not overcome. It is not just, therefore, that thine image should be placed above that of Rameses, since thou hast not surpassed him by thy deeds."

At the words of this aged priest, inspired with a patriotic remembrance as though by the breath of his god, Darius, the undisputed sovereign of twenty satrapies whose chiefs had kings for vassals, bowed his head in silence and abandoned his haughty design.

Royal cartouche of
Rameses Mei-Amoun.

APPENDIX.

APPENDIX.

I.

THE CUSHITES, (page 15.)

... THE Coptic idiom, a remnant of the old Egyptian tongue, is incontestably one of the most curious although one of the most meagre fragments of the languages of antiquity. An original kinship with the Semitic idioms has been discovered for it; since the Semitic dialects have penetrated the old Cushite foundation of human tongues. . . . .

Although the Coptic is the antipodes of the Sanscrit, a thousand reasons seem to conspire to make us look in the basin of the Indus for the seat of primitive civilization transported to the valley of the Nile at an epoch preceding the time when Southern Asia was wrested from the Cushites by the Aryan and Semitic races. If we find in the popular forms of worship of India the contrast between which and the religious notions of the Vedas is so marked, a strong resemblance to the creeds of Egypt, is there any reason to feel surprised when we discover some words in Coptic that have an equivalent in the Sanscrit? There is one thing that must never be lost sight of, in any inquiry relative to those distant times. It is absurd to say: this is of Indian and that of Egyptian origin, for the influences that shaped them have followed the tide of migration.

Thus, even while admitting the influence of the Arian and

Semitic creeds upon the forms of Egyptian worship, we cannot avoid recognizing in certain portions of the Vedas a character common to the religion of Egypt. The cause of these coincidences must be sought in the primitive extension of the race of Cush and of Shem in the regions lying in the immediate vicinity of the Aryan tribes. (Baron Eckstein, *Researches concerning Primitive Humanity.*)

II.

THE TEMPLE OF DENDERAH, (p. 29.)

THE great celebrity conferred on this monument since the French expedition of 1798, is associated with an archæological error respecting the date of a planisphere carved on the ceiling of the temple, and with the fantastic speculations of Dupuis and his school on this pretended relic of antiquity. Nevertheless, the ruins of *Tentyris*, of which the wretched village of Denderah retains the name with its Arabic modification, have in themselves a real interest, principally owing to the state of preservation in which the temple is found.

But, if this temple be one of the best preserved in Egypt, it is also one of the most recent. Commenced under the last Ptolemies it was not completed until some time in Nero's reign. The most ancient names that figure on the hieroglyphic inscriptions are those of Cleopatra and of her son Ptolemy Cæsarion; the latest is that of Nero. A Greek inscription legible upon the upper part of the portico, on the overhanging of the cornice, is in the name of Tiberius and dated in the 21st year of his sovereignty.

The emperors Caligula and Claudius also contributed to the embellishments of the edifice. Near the hieroglyphic inscription in which are read the names of Cleopatra and of the son she bore to Cæsar, on the external part of the rear wall of the temple, there is carved a portrait of that famous Queen ; it does but little credit to the chisel of the artist. The whole sculptural work, moreover, betrays a period of decadence in the art. The hieroglyphics, like the ornaments, are of inferior execution, as we find them on many other monuments of the same periods. But architecture maintained itself better in the midst of this wasting away of art. Here, for instance, the general effect, notwithstanding the bad taste and the heaviness of detail, lacks neither grandeur nor majesty, and the temple, even in its present condition, still produces a vivid impression on the traveller.

The portico or *pronaos*, a work of Tiberius, is supported by 24 columns in four rows of six columns each. An intercolumnary wall, breast high, extending between the pillars, closes the lower part of the first row. The ceiling, which is in complete preservation, is ornamented with the celebrated zodiac which has been the subject of so many dissertations and hypotheses. To the portico succeed three halls of unequal size, the first adorned with columns, and the two others with adjoining side rooms. On the ceiling of one of these chambers was secured a planisphere which is now in Paris. The *naos* or sanctuary which terminates this range of halls is isolated by a circular passage from the six rooms that surround it. The total length of the temple is 81 and its width 34 yards. That of the portico, which overshoots the body of the temple in such manner as to give the whole structure the form of a T, is 43 yards in length by 98 of interior height. The temple was preceded by its *dromos*, extending a length of 110 paces to an isolated pylon which bears the names of Domitian and of Trajan.

This temple was dedicated to the goddess Hathor, from whom the city, to all appearance, had taken its name (*Than-athor*—the habitation of Hathor.) In the inscriptions distributed in various parts of the temple, the goddess bears, among other titles, that of the Queen of Tenathyr, a word from which, in the fullness of time, was derived *Tentyris*. In its turn the latter degenerated to *Denderah*.

M. de Rougé, in one of his lectures at the college of France, in the course of 1865, communicated to his audience a letter from M. Mariette, announcing the discovery that the latter had just made, beneath the temple of Denderah, of a subterranean chapel, the construction of which the indefatigable explorer thought that he could trace back to Cheops, (*Chuffu.*) the founder of the Great Pyramid. Whatever may be the credit to assign or the reservations to be made in reference to this opinion, one thing is certain, to wit, that the discovery, in itself, does not in any degree affect the relatively modern dates of the upper temple and of its zodiac. The utmost it could do would be to give fresh credit to the hypothesis (rather quickly abandoned by the savants of our day) according to which the first religious monuments of Egypt were subterranean temples.

III.

THE ANCIENT BED OF THE NILE, (p. 33.)

To the westward of the Delta, parallel to its line of inclination and thirty-five miles distant, runs a valley that opens on the Mediterranean Sea not far from Arabs Cape. The name *Bahr-bela-ma* given by the wandering tribes to this valley signifies the *river without water;* it stretches far away toward the south and sends off many side valleys to the Nile below Gizeh, (the Bahr-el-Farigh,) and toward Fayoum. It is one of the singular features of the physical configuration of Northeastern Africa. A simple crest or ridge separates it from the *Wadi-Natroun* or the valley of the lakes of Natron, which no doubt was only one of its branches at the period when the waters rolled full and high between its banks fully 15,000 yards apart. The Bahr-bela-Ma is clogged with sand. Neither vegetation nor springs can be seen;

but, on the other hand there are such great quantities of petrified trunks of trees as are met with between the Mokattan and the Red Sea. Some of these trunks, completely transformed to stone, are as much as eight or ten yards in length. Impressions of fossil fish have also been noticed on the stone, and it has been ascertained that the pebbles picked up there belong to the primitive mountains of Upper Egypt and the high Ethiopian Plains. These petrifactions are to be found, also, in the Bahr-el-Farigh.

Ascending southward across the Fayoum, the small oasis, the interior oasis and that of Khargeh, one may follow the traces of the Bahr-bela-ma to the bosom of the Nubian deserts as far as those *wadys* which, traversed by the roads leading to Darfur between the 20th and the 22nd degrees of latitude, seem to weld themselves to the most salient angles of the present bed of the Nile to the northward of Dongola. The Bahr-bela-ma is, then, but the old channel followed by the waters of the Ethiopian plateaux ere the convulsions of the crust of the earth had opened an outlet for them toward the primitive gulf which became Egypt, thanks to the local depressions of the surface.

IV.

THE SHEPHERD KING APAPSAS AND THE GOD SOUTEKE.

WE read in Strabo that "at Heliopolis and Memphis there were edifices of a barbarian order of architecture, with several rows of columns, but with neither ornaments nor designs." Was not the temple reared to Soutekh, *the only God*, by the Semitic iconoclast Apapias, one of these edifices? Is it any other than the monument without ornament, without sculpture, without a single letter, discovered by M. Mariette twenty yards from the great Sphinx of Gizeh, and in which a well filled up with the statues of the gods and the kings of the fourth dynasty, bears witness to the hatred of the founder for the idols and fetiches of the preceding generations?

V.

THE NAMES OF RAMESES II.

[Note by M. Rougé.]

If the testimony of Tacitus placed the present reading of the name of Rameses beyond dispute it did not assist us in comprehending how the Greeks had come to write a name so different from it. The condition in which the royal lists taken from Manetho have reached us still increase the embarrassment. In the nineteenth dynasty no other name had been found on these lists than the genuine Egyptian one of *Rameses Mei-Amoun*. The Greek chronologists who have transmitted these lists to us felt that they could not omit introducing the Sesostris of Herodotus, somewhere. A list of the Egyptian kings on which Sesostris had not been named would have seemed to them something as monstrous as a history of Greece from which the name of Alexander had been excluded. Hence these compilers of quotations found in Manetho, at the twelfth dynasty, a king whose name *Sesortasen* presented some analogy to that of *Sesostris*. Moreover, he was a conqueror. His monuments, which still exist to this day, show that he had advanced the frontiers of Egypt on the Nubian side, and that his memory was still held in sufficient honor to cause fresh temples to be reared to his memory many centuries after his death. Undoubtedly there were in the first extracts from Manetho some words of praise following this royal name, as there were after several others; and this circumstance, joined to the similarity of names, induced the chronologists to place the Sesostris of the Greeks just there. The writing that accompanies it is, moreover, too clear in its specifications to be accepted as the genuine **text of Manetho.**

APPENDIX. 255

It is not the Sesostris of Herodotus that we meet with, then, at the twelfth dynasty; it was, indeed, a king who was victorious on the frontiers, but whose armies had never penetrated into Asia, and this false application of the legend of Sesostris may have been caused by the complete absence of that famous name from the real lists of Manetho. Since the British Museum published its fine collection of papyri, all Egyptian scholars have remarked in the historical texts of the nineteenth dynasty a singular royal monogram which reads *Sesu*, [hieroglyph cartouche]. The same name is also found at Thebes on a mural inscription. It seemed impossible to find any particular place for this king *Sesu*, and the analogy of the name with *Sesostris* was so tempting, that it no doubt occurred to the mind of more than one archæologist; but the question was to find some decisive information so as to correctly place the king designated by the device. I believe that I have been so fortunate as to come across the proof desired, in the Egyptian collection in the imperial musuem at Vienna.

That museum possesses a small solid pyramid of calcareous stone; its four sides are covered with finely executed carvings. I have described, in the catalogue of the Louvre, the ordinary decoration of this small monument. It is, so to speak, turned so as to face eastwardly, and is always made up of invocations to the sun in his various positions. The Vienna pyramid does not fall short of this programme, and these repeated invocations have supplied opportunities to frequently mention the name of the person dedicating it. That personage was called, like the great king, *Rameses Mei-Amoun*, [hieroglyphs]. Excepting the border surrounding the royal name, the signs are exactly the same. Now, twice upon the pyramid, the same Egyptian is named

APPENDIX.

simply *Ses*, 𓂉𓂉 written without the vowel. A third time his name is written *Ses Mei-Amoun* 𓂉𓂉𓄿𓏤 in such manner as to make us perfectly understand that *Ses* is a popular abbreviation of *Rameses*. This royal name, in its most complete form, that which was particularly in use under Rameses I.,

reads thus : ⊙𓂉𓏤𓅆 *Ramesesu*. From this form are derived several abbreviations. On the historical papyri

we find the scrolls  *Sesu*,

Sesesu, and ⊙𓂉𓅆 *Ra-Sesesu*, all used indifferently to designate Rameses II. I have even found there the

variation 𓂉𓏤𓅆𓄿𓏤 *Sesu-Mei-Amoun*, identical with that which is read once on the pyramid at Vienna, where the surname *Mei-Amoun* accompanies the abbreviation of the proper name. It is certain, then, that there did exist a popular abbreviation *Sesu*, so currently used to designate the great Rameses, that it could be employed indifferently to write the title of one of his namesakes. The form used in the papyri *Sesesu* is very exactly what Diodorus has transcribed into *Sesoosis*. It is not that I regard the form *Sesostris* as less correct; it may be derived from the scroll *Ra-Sesesu*. The Egyptians had known a number of kings whose names ended in the word *ra*, or sun (pronounced *ri* by iotacism, according to all the Greek transcripts, in the terminations). Although the sign for the sun ⊙ was traced at the commencement of the scroll as an honorary distinction, the grammatical construction frequently brought it to the end of the name. It is thus that the name of king Menkeres, written invariably [cartouche] *Re-men-ke*, became in the pronunciation [glyphs] and it is in this way that I found it written

Men   ke   re

and it is in this way that I found it written for the proper name of a Saitic functionary. It seems to me very probable that, in consequence of this custom, the abbreviation [cartouche] became transformed in the mouth of the people to *Sesesu-ri* and that it was in this shape that they peated, in the presence of Herodotus, the name that produced the Greek from *Sesostris*.

[Extract from the *Athæneum français*, 1856.]

VI.

THE IMAGES OF ANCESTORS, (p. 79.)

THE small statues of the ancestors and predecessors of Rameser II., which the musal paintings represent as figuring at the panegyric of his coronation, are only thirteen in number. They are, besides those of his father Seti and his grandfather Rameses I., those of nine lawful kings of the 18th dynasty. Aahmes, Amenoph I., Thothmes I., Thothmes II., Amenoph II., Thothmes IV., Amenoph III., and Horemheb. These historical sovereigns are preceded by a Mentu Hotep VI., of the 11th dynasty, who has left no trace of his personality on the monuments, and of the legendary Mena— two personages only, and problematical at that, to represent the long series of ages attributed to the history of Egypt beyond the time of the Hycsos ! .... Is it not as though, in a gallery of portraits of the Bourbon race, no place had been found prior to the time of Henry IV., for any but the likenesses of Robert the Strong and Francis the son of Hector ?

This leads us naturally to some reflections on the tables or lists of the Egyptian Kings recently discovered and published.

THE TABLES OF ABYDOS AND OF MEMPHIS.

In the month of September, 1863, M. Mariette, who had just made some excavations in the great burial district of Sakkara near Memphis with great success, published in the *Archæological Review* (Revue Archéologique) a monumental table containing, in their order, the names of the fifty-three Pharaohs. Seti I., of the 19th dynasty, himself, comprised in the same table, is represented as making the offerings prescribed by the funereal rites, to his deified predecessors. Although the Egyptian scribes to whom was confided the task of recalling their names, have inverted the order of the kings of the 12th dynasty, whether through inattention or in pursuance of some purpose as yet unfathomed, in such manner as to ascend instead of descending the scale of time; and although this table contains among the kings of the first dynasties, some names until then unknown, still, such as it is, it was at the time of its publication, in the month of September 1863, the most important document of its kind that had seen the light since the discovery of the famous tablet of Abydos in the possession of the British Museum. But it was not long ere the glory of this discovery was eclipsed by another, still more important, found by the indefatigable French explorer. M. Mariette was very recently lucky enough to find a considerable portion of a temple, buried in the soil and dedicated to Asiris, in the heart of the holy city of Abydos, the same from which the table in the British Museum came. Upon one of the walls of this

APPENDIX. 259

temple he discovered a representation of the offerings made by Seti I., and by his son, (who, afterwards, was Rameses the Great,) to their deceased ancestors, no less than seventy-six in number, from the first dynasty ruler, Menes, down to Sethi himself. This discovery, which a German doctor, a savant by trade and a robber by calling, who clung to the steps of M. Mariette, has tried to take away from our countryman, is undoubtedly of great value, but has perhaps been rated too high in a historical point of view. A slight observation will suffice to prove as much. The first part of the old table of Abydos having been destroyed, it is not known whether this table did or did not commence with Menes. The Sakkara tablet does not contain this name, which, however, is found upon the new list of Abydos. These three lists are of nearly the same epoch; the first, dating from Rameses the Great, contains 49 kings; the second and the third are of the reign of Seti, and yet do not present the same number of names. The temple of Memphis has fifty two; that of Abydos seventy-five—all predecessors of the same Seti. Hence it must be inferred that the Egyptian priests who prepared them, had the privilege of selecting the kings whose names they wished, to retain a choice the motives of which must frequently have varied, since the two tables of the same city of Abydos, composed at two periods quite close together, differ in the names as well as in the number of them.

But it will be confessed that the choice made by the historian of certain kings commendable for their virtues or odious for their vices is reasonable only when one knows the motives that determined this adoption or exclusion, and all becomes mystery to one who has not possession of the key to the labyrinth. On the other hand, isolated monuments and the list of the royal chamber at Karnak have revealed to us the existence in Upper Egypt of dynasties of Nantefs and Sevekhoteps, preceding the 12th dynasty; and, although localized, perhaps, in Upper Egypt, they were powerful, but the names of all their people are omitted on the three tables of which we are treating.

APPENDIX.

A careful comparative examination of these different doc uments casts a ray of light, however, upon the dark places. By its help, we perceive that there was a period when the priests had not the privilege of choosing among the names of the kings ; there was, indeed, a period in the history of Egypt in relation to which the different tables agree with each other as they, likewise, agree with the lists of the historian Manetho. This epoch was the commencement of the famous 12th dynasty of the *Sesortasens* and of the *Amenemhas*. In ascending from Rameses II. to Amenemha I. everything is clear, everything follows in the same order on the different documents ; but, in taking the last named king for the point of departure, all becomes doubt and confusion excepting at the epoch, comparatively free from clouds and mists, of the Pharaohs who built the great pyramids. Hence we may conclude that the learned copyists and scribes of the colleges at Thebes and Memphis composed, in the fourteenth century preceding the Christian Era, a history of Egypt in which the whole period anterior to the 12th dynasty is but a tissue of fables, legends and traditions toned down to the historic form,—something like the history of England written in the ninth and tenth centuries by monks and translated into Latin by Geoffrey of Monmouth. The papyrus at Turin is a collection of this nature, with its mythical kings, its divine dynasties and its legendary conquerors and law-givers. The history of Manetho is probably but an abridgment or an amplification of these traditions, and, thus, these compilations of the fourteenth century before our era bring no support to the history of Manetho in all that concerns the epochs anterior to the commencement of the 12th dynasty. And, in fact, it is with this period that Manetho himself opens the second book of his history and emerges from the confused eras of the unfamiliar dynasties and nameless kings in order to enter upon the historically and monumentally well ascertained series of kings belonging to the 12th dynasty.

The conclusion of all this reasoning is self-apparent. The

history of the Egyptian Kings of the united monarchies of Thebes and Memphis begins with the 12th dynasty; with its accession the tide of Egyptian history brightens; the priests retain without difficulty a remembrance of the kings that had governed the whole country, whereas previously they had seen before them a crowd of local sovereigns, of mere chiefs of cities and of petty kings independent of each other—a confused throng from which they chose whom they pleased according to the different degrees of renown that each of these petty princes had been able to acquire in the different great centres of the theocratic power. Some of these Pharaohs, the most celebrated for instance of those who reared the Pyramids, and the old King Papi, are inscribed, alone and the same time, upon the lists of Upper and Lower Egypt. But the inscription of the name of Menes, the legendary founder of the empire, upon the Theban list of Abydos, and his exclusion from the Memphian list of Sakkara, confirm the opinion that we owe what we have of Egyptian history in form to the labors of the Theban writers belonging to the palmy time of Egyptian literature, the age of the Pharaohs of the dynasty of Rameses.

VII.

THE ARMY OF RAMESES II—THE MILITARY CASTE, (p. 98.)

THE figures given by Diodorus (Book I., ch. 54) for the army of *Sesoosis* (Rameses) are 600,000 foot-soldiers, 24,000 horsemen and 27,000 chariots. The only specimen of horsemanship that has been discovered on all the monuments explored in old Egypt, from Memphis to the Cataracts, is a veritable caricature, viz., a terrified fugitive twisting and struggling on the back of a runaway horse. Diodorus says elsewhere (Book I., ch. 31,) that, in his time, the population of Egypt ran up to 3,000,000 of souls, and that it had been millions under the Ptolemies. This last estimate, without being impossible, seems very small when compared with the cultivable surface of the country, even putting the latter at its highest estimate. The actual number of 2,900,000 already surpasses the average population of France in respect to the extent of its territory. It is true that in the time of the Pharaohs and the Ptolemies, the cultivable surface of Egypt may have been double what it is now, and this would give us, all proportions carefully observed, a total of 6,000,000 souls. In his "*Memoirs Dictated at Saint Helena*," the former general of the army of the East pretends that under good administration, when irrigating canals extended from the valley of the Nile to the Oasis of Libya, this number may have risen to 10 millions. But did a foundation for this hypothesis ever really exist?

However that may have been, here is what Herodotus has told us of the military caste in Egypt:

Euterpe CLXIV. . . . The warriors receive from their countrymen the names of Calasiries and Hermotybies. They live in the *nomes* hereinafter enumerated, and all Egypt is divided into *nomes*.

CLXV. Those of the Hermotybies are: Busiris, Sais, Chemnis, Papremis, the island of Prosopitis and the half of Natho; the Hermotybies have their domains upon these nomes: their number is one hundred and sixty thousand men when they are complete. Not one of them has ever learned any of the mechanical arts, but they devote themselves to the military profession.

CLXVI. The nomes of the Calasiries were Thebes, Bubastis, Aphris, Thanis, Mendes, Sebennys, Athribis, Pharbetis, Thmuis, Onuphis, Anysis, Mycephoris; the last named nome occupies an island opposite Bubastis; the Calasiries have their domains on these nomes. Their number is two hundred and fifty thousand when they are in their full muster. They are not permitted to cultivate any mechanical art, but they practice the arts of war and hand them down from father to son.

CLXVII. I cannot decide with certainty whether the

Greeks have received these usages from the Egyptians, since I perceive that the Thracians, the Scythians, the Persians, the Lydians, and nearly all the barbarians place such of their citizens as have learned the mechanical arts, and their descendants after them, in the lowermost rank in their estimation, and considered those the noblest of men who free themselves from manual labor, and especially those who resort to warlike service. Such were the ideas of all the Greeks, especially of the Lacedæmonians; the Corinthians were they who least despised the artisan.

CLXVIII. The following privileges were assigned to the soldiers, and they were the only Egyptians, excepting the priests, to whom anything of the kind was ever granted. Each of them possesses twelve roods of excellent land exempt from taxation. The Egyptian rood is equivalent to a square lot measuring a hundred cubits on each side, the cubit being identical with that of Samos. Such are their privileges. They also enjoy by turns, and never twice the same, these other advantages: every year a thousand Calasiries and as many Hermotybies form the king's guard; to these, besides their land, are given every day five mini of baked bread, two mini of beef and four cups of wine.

VIII.

THE ROBUS, (p. 126.)

WE are not unaware that Dr. Brugsch, and with him many other Egyptian scholars, make this people out to have been a tribe in the north of Africa. For them, *Robus* meant *Libus* or *Libyans*. But notwithstanding the scientific authority of these learned men, we do not think that Libyan shepherds ever wore the double garment and the long tunic which the mural paintings attribute to the Robus, along with their clear complexion, their blue eyes and light beard. Neither do we admit that any kind of a confederation of nomadic tribes to the westward of the Nile ever was importan: enough to have abandoned from 12,000 to 13,000 corpses to the Egyptian soldiers on one field of battle to be mutilated, as the inscriptions at Medinet-Abou pretend in reference to the Robus.

For all these reasons, it remains quite evident to us, as it was for Champollion and for Wilkinson, that it will not do to rank the Robus among the Eastern peoples, and that they occupied in Asia a country very remote from Egypt, and enjoyed a climate much more temperate than that of the borders of the Nile.

IX.

MANNERS AND CUSTOMS OF THE EGYPTIANS.

[Extracts from Herodotus.]

XXXV. . . . The Egyptians live beneath a sky peculiar to themselves; their country is watered by a river different from all other rivers: and then they have established laws and customs which are, for the most part, the opposite of those of the rest of human beings. With them the women go to market and trade; the men stay at home and weave. Everywhere else the weavers pass the woof above, the Egyptians pass it below. The men carry burthens on their heads, the women carry them on their shoulders. No woman has the office of priesthood for gods of either sex; the men only can be priests. The young men are never constrained to support their parents, if such be not their own wish; but the girls are compelled to do so even against their will.

XXXVI. Elsewhere the priests of the gods wear long hair: in Egypt they shave; among other men, the custom is to cut the hair when mourning commences for any near relative; the Egyptians, to show respect for the dead, let the hair and the beard which previously they shaved off, grow on their heads and under their chins. Other men live separate from their animals; the Egyptians live pell mell with them. Elsewhere, wheat and barley are staples of food, but the Egyptians consider it a disgrace to live upon that diet; they use *dourah*. They knead dough with their feet and clay with their hands, and they lift manure with both hands.... Every man wears two garments; the woman has only one. Other people fasten the rings and the cables of their sails inside; the Egyptians fasten them outside. The Greeks write and count from left to right; the Egyptians go from right to left, and, in doing so, claim that they go to the right, and the Greeks to the left. They have two kinds of letters—the sacred and the vulgate characters.*

XXXVII. As they are observers of ceremonies more than other men they practise the following customs: they drink from a brazen cup which they cleanse every day; and this not some only but all of them do. They wear linen garments, and are very careful to have them always fresh and clean. They deem it better to be neat than to be handsome. Every three days, the priests shave their whole bodies, so that no vermin may defile them while they are serving the gods. They wear nothing but linen garments and shoes of papyrus bark, and they are not permitted to use others. They wash themselves with fresh water twice each day and twice each night. They accomplish other rites innumerable one might say, but they enjoy uncommon advantages. They neither wear out nor spend what belongs to them; sacred viands are cooked for them; every day plenty of beef and geese are sent to them; grape wine is distributed to them; but, at the same time, they cannot eat fish. No beans are planted throughout all Egypt, and if any come up they are not eaten, either raw or cooked. The priests cannot bear the sight of

---

* The hieroglyphics and demotic characters.

them, since they look upon the vegetable as impure. Each god is served not by one priest only, but by several, one of whom is the high priest, and when he dies his son succeeds him.

XLVII. The Egyptians regard the hog as an impure animal. Consequently, should one of them, in passing near a pig, be touched by him, he is made to go down into the river without undressing, and they bathe him in his clothing; on the other hand, the Egyptian swineherds only, among all the population, cannot enter any temple in the country. No one gives them his daughters in marriage and no one marries their daughters, nor can they intermarry excepting among themselves. The Egyptians do not think it proper to sacrifice a pig to any other deities than the Moon and Bacchus;* to them only they sacrifice that animal, at the same moment, during the full Moon, and eat the flesh of the victim. The manner of making this sacrifice of swine is as follows: when the victim has been slaughtered, they fasten together the extremity of the tail, the spleen and the kidneys. These are then wrapped in all the fat found in the stomach, and are burned upon the altar. The remainder of the flesh is eaten during the same day at the close of the sacrifice: no one would taste it on any other day.

XLVIII. At the evening repast, on the day previous to the festival of Bacchus, (Asiri,) every man, in front of his own door, having slaughtered a young pig gives it to the swineherd who had sold it to him, to take away. The Egyptians celebrate the rest of the festival as the Greeks do, in all but the music and the singing.

. . . L. Nearly all the names of the gods came to Greece from Egypt. My researches prove to me that we get them from the barbarian countries, and I think that they come especially from Egypt. Excepting Neptune and the Dioscuri, of whom I have already spoken; excepting Juno, Vesta, Themis, the Graces and the Nereids. The names of all the

---
* Isis and Asiri.

other gods have always existed among the Egyptians. I here repeat what they themselves declared to me. The divinities of whom they say they do not know the names seem to me to have been named by the Pelasgi, excepting Neptune (Poseidon). The Libyans were they who revealed this last divinity to us: no one pronounced his name previously, and they have always honored him as a god. The Egyptians do not worship heroes.

LI. The Greeks have learned from the Egyptians the customs which I have already mentioned and others that I shall speak of hereafter.

LII. Primitively, the Pelasgi, when praying, made offerings of all kinds to their gods, as I was told at Dodona, but they gave neither name nor surname to any one of them; for they had never heard any given to them. They called them gods for the sole reason that, after having put the universe in order, they maintained all its laws. Then, much time having elapsed, they learned from Egypt the names of gods other than Bacchus, and, a long time afterward, this last name too. They consulted the oracle of Dodona in relation to these names, that being the one which the Greeks consider the most ancient, and which, at that time, was the only one. When the Pelasgi had asked whether they should accept names coming from the barbarians, the oracle replied "Take them!" Thereupon, they sacrificed to the gods under these names, of which they made use from that time forth, and, finally, the Greeks received the same from them.

LIII. Whence came each of the gods? Have they always existed? What is the form of them? Nothing of all this was known, properly speaking, until a very recent period. For I think that Hesiod and Homer only four hundred years anterior to me, not more. Well, it was they who made up the Greek theogony; who gave names to the gods; who distributed honors and attributes among them; who described their forms, and it appears to me that the poets said to have preceded those two men were born after them.

LVIII The oracle of Thebes in Egypt and that of Dodona

yield their responses in nearly the same manner. The art of prophesying from an inspection of the victims came also from Egypt. The Egyptians were the first of all men to establish solemn processions, holidays and offerings, and it is from them that the Greeks learned these ceremonies. This, for me, is proof of the fact: in Egypt it is plain that they are very ancient, and, in Greece that they have been but recently established.

LIX. The Egyptians do not restrict themselves every year to one solemn festival only; those great assemblages are frequent. The first of these and the one which is the most zealously attended, is held at Bubastis in honor of Diana: the second at Busiris in honor of Isis, since in this city stands the largest temple of Isis. The city itself is built in the midst of the Delta, and Isis, in the language of the Greeks, is Ceres. The third gathering is at Sais in honor of Minerva: the fourth at Heliopolis, in honor of the Sun; the fifth at Buto, in honor of Latona; the sixth at Papremis, in honor of Mars.

LX. And this is the way in which they repair to the City of Bubastis, for both men and women go thither, in great multitudes, from all parts, each family in its boat. Some of the women have castanets and sound them: for their part during the whole trip some of the men play the flute and the remainder of both sexes clap their hands and sing. When, as they sail along, they approach one of the cities that dot the way, they moor the boat and do what I am going to relate. Among the women some continue their singing or rattle their castanets, while others with loud cries jeer at the women of the city, and others again dance. . . . At each town on the river banks, they do in like manner. On their arrival at Bubastis, the passengers begin to celebrate the festival and offer sacrifices; and in this solemnity they consume more grape wine than during all the rest of the year. Without counting the children, more than seven hundred thousand men and women, according to the statements of the inhabitants, assemble there. Such are the things that take place at Bubastis.

LXI .... After the sacrifices, the men and women, thronging together in a numberless multitude, ply each other with blows. For what god they strike it would be an impiety in me to tell. The Carians established in Egypt do that and more still ; they cut each other's foreheads with knives ; by that they show that they are strangers and not Egyptians.

LXII. When the latter are assembled to make sacrifices in the city of Sais, during a certain night, they all light, in in the open air around their houses, a great number of lamps filled with salt and oil, the wick floating on the surface.

The wick burns all night, and this celebration is called the " festival of the lamps." Such Egyptians as have not come to the assemblage equally celebrate the night of the sacrifice ; all light their lamps as well, so that it is not the city of Sais alone that is illuminated, but all Egypt. For what reason has this night its share of illuminations and honors ? That is told in a sacred legend.

LXIII. At Heliopolis, at Buto, the celebrants restrict themselves to the immolation of victims. At Papremis, the same sacrifices are offered up and the same ceremonies are observed as in the other cities ; Moreover, when the sun begins to wane, some of the priests are busied around the statue ; others in much greater number, armed with staves, take their stations at the entrance of the temple ; the people, that is to say many thousand persons, fulfilling their vows and similarly armed, are assembled on the opposite side. Now, on the previous evening, the statue, enclosed in a small chapel of painted wood, had been carried from the temple to another station ; the priests that had been placed around the statue go to work and draw a four-wheeled chariot to convey the wooden chapel and the statue that it contains back to the large temple ; but those who are in the portico refuse to admit them. The crowd of devotees, rushing to the rescue of the god, strike them ; they defend themselves; a violent conflict with sticks and staves ensues, and many a head is broken; however, the Egyptians declare that no one has ever been killed.

.... LXV. But the Egyptians observe with extreme attention all the prescribed forms of religion, and particularly those that I am about to describe. Although coterminous with Libya, their country is not infested with wild beasts. The animals that they know are all reputed sacred, those that do and those that do not live with men, alike. Were I to tell why they hold them sacred, I should, in my narrative, penetrate to things divine of which I am seeking to avoid saying a word, for if I have chanced to touch upon them, I have not done so without being forced to it by necessity. There exists, on the subject of animals, a custom which I am about to set forth; keepers of the two sexes are appointed to feed each kind separately; the son succeeds the father in this honorific office. The inhabitants of the towns fulfill their vows through the medium of these keepers; when they have made a vow to the divinity to which one of these animals belongs, they shave either the whole head, or half of it, or the third part of the head of their sons; they then put in the scales of a balance, on one side the hair, and on the other its weight in silver; and, whatever that weight may be, they give it to the keeper of the animal. The latter in return cuts up some fish in pieces and throws them to his animals for fodder: such is the food offered to them. Should any person kill one of these animals wilfully, he is put to death; should he kill unintentionally, he is punished with a fine fixed by the priests. Any one killing an ibis or a sparrow-hawk voluntarily or involuntarily would infallibly be immolated.

LXVI. Whatever may be the number of the animals fed along with the men, it would be still more considerable if, in the cat species, for instance, the males did not destroy a great many of the young by savage instinct, or if frequent fires did not kill a vast number of these creatures. When such accidents occur, profound grief takes possession of the

Egyptians. When, in any dwelling, a cat dies naturally, the inhabitants shave off their eyebrows only; but if it be a dog that dies they shave their bodies and their heads.

LXVII. Dead cats are taken to consecrated buildings; then, after having been embalmed, they are buried at Bubastis. Dogs are buried, each one in its own town, in consecrated chambers, and ichneumons the same. The shrew-mice and the sparrowhawks are taken to Buto, the ibis to Hermopolis. Bears, which are very rarely met with, and wolves (jackals rather) whose size does not exceed that of foxes, are interred on the spot where they are found lying dead.

LXVIII. The crocodile during the four coldest months eats nothing; although a quadruped, it lives both on land and water; it lays its eggs on land and hatches them there. It passes the greater part of the day on the banks and the whole night in the river because the water is warmer than the open air and the dew. Of all the perishable creatures that we know this one reaches the largest from the smallest bulk; its eggs are no bigger than those of a goose; the young one is born only the length of the egg and grows to seventeen cubits,—sometimes more. It has eyes like a pig, large teeth, and jutting scales all along the dorsal column. It is the only animal that has no tongue. Its lower jaw is immovable, and it closes the upper jaw upon it, in this too being peculiar among all living creatures. It has strong claws, and on its back scales which cannot be cut. Blind in the water, on land its sight is piercing; and, as it passes the most of the time in the river, its mouth is full of insects that suck its blood. Animals and birds flee from it, but the *trochylus* lives in amity with it because that bird renders it good service. In fact when the crocodile comes out of the water and reaches dry land, its first need is to inhale the breath of the zephyr; it emerges, therefore, with its jaws wide open; then, the trochylus has access to them and can relieve it of the insects which it swallows. The crocodile receives this relief with joy, and never harms the trochylus.

LXIX. To some Egyptians, the crocodile is sacred; to others it is not: the latter treat it as an enemy. Around Thebes and Lake Mœris, the inhabitants consider it sacred. Each one of them rears a crocodile, which is tamed by training, and they hang pendants and buckles of crystal and gold in its ears; they encircle its fore-paws with bracelets and give it choice viands from the sacrifices. In fine, while it is alive they tend it the best they can; when it is dead they embalm it and bury it in consecrated ground. On the contrary, the inhabitants of the territory of Elephantine eat crocodiles, not regarding them as sacred in any wise. The Egyptian name of this animal is not *crocodile*, but *champse*. The Ionians have called it crocodile, finding it resemble in shape the lizards (*krokodeilos*) which breed in stone walls.

LXXVII. The Egyptians who inhabit the cultivated part of the country, taking pleasure in adorning their remembrance, are the most refined of all the men whom I approached and studied. Their regimen is as follows: very careful in the preservation of their health they purge themselves with emetics and clysters every month for three days in succession, since they think that all the diseases of man come from his food and drink. Aside from these precautions the Egyptians are, next to the Libyans, the healthiest of mortals, in my opinion owing to the steadiness of their seasons; in fact, sickness comes upon us, in consequence of the changes of all things, especially of the seasons. They feed on bread made from *dourrah;* they drink a wine made from barley, in those districts where there are no vines. They eat fish, some of it dried in the sun, other kinds cured in drying-houses, close by the sea. Among birds, they prefer quails and ducks, and besides these, some small birds dried raw. All other birds and fish that they have in their country, apart from those which they consider sacred, form part of their food, roasted or boiled.

LXVIII. At the banquets of the wealthy, when the eating is over, a man brings in a coffin, the wooden effigy of a dead body perfectly imitated by the sculptor and the painter, and one or two cubits in length. This the man shows to each of the guests, and, as he does so, he says: "Look upon this; then drink and be merry, for such as thou seest it wilt thou be, after thy death."

LXXX. With the Lacedemonians only do the Egyptians agree in this other custom: young men when they meet their elders, yield the path and pass aside to make way for them; at their approach they rise from their seats. But in what follows, they do not resemble any Hellenic nation. Instead of saluting with the voice on the street, they do so by letting their hand fall to the knee.

LXXXI. They dress in linen tunics with fringes around their legs; they call these fringes *calisiris*, and over the tunics they wear mantles of white wool. However, they do not enter the temples with the woolen garment on; nor are these left on corpses to be buried with them that would be an act of impiety. In this respect, they chime in with the Orphic, or, as they are likewise called, the Bacchic traditions, which are equally observed by the Egyptians and by the Pythagoreans, since among the latter it is an impious act to bury in woolen tissues any one who has been initiated in the mysteries. A religious motive is ascribed to this custom.

LXXXIV. In Egypt, the practice of medicine is divided into specialities, each physician devoting himself to one branch of disease, and not to several. Physicians swarm everywhere, some for the eyes, others for the head, others for the teeth, others for the stomach, and still others for internal disorders.

LXXXV. Their acts of mourning and their funeral ceremonies are after this fashion: when they lose a relative whom they greatly esteemed, all the women of the family, after having bedaubed their heads and faces with mire, leave the dead body in the house and wander hither and thither through the town, beating their uncovered breasts and naked bosoms, in company with all those who hold relations of friendship with them. On the other hand, the men with uncovered breasts beat themselves in the same manner; this done, they bear the body away to embalm it.

LXXXVI. There are persons entrusted with this business. It forms their profession. When the corpse has been brought to them, the embalmers show the friends of the deceased wooden models of corpses, imitated in painting, and they point out those that they consider the most worthy of attention, the name* of which I do not deem it proper to give in this place; they then exhibit the second, which costs less, and finally the third, which is the cheapest of all. After this, they ask how they are desired to operate upon the corpse, and so soon as they agree upon the style and the terms the relatives depart. The operators thus left to themselves proceed in the following manner to embalm in the best style. First, with a bent iron, they extract the brain through the nostrils, at least the greater part of it, and afterward the rest by the application of dissolvent injections. Then, with a sharpened Ethiopian stone, they cut open the sides of the corpse, take out all the intestines from the abdomen, wash the latter with palm wine, besprinkle it with powdered perfumes, and at last sew it up, after having filled it with bruised myrrh of pure quality, cinnamon and other perfumes, from among which incense alone is excluded. These operations completed, they dry the body in carbonate of soda and leave it plunged in that for seventy days, but no longer; they are not permitted to do so. At the expiration of these seventy days, they wash the corpse and wrap it up completely in bandages of the finest linen saturated with gum, of which the Egyptians make great use instead of glue. The relatives then again take possession of the corpse, enclose it in a wooden case shaped like a human body, and place it standing against the wall in the burial chamber. This is the costliest style of embalming.

LXXXVII. For those who prefer the middle method of embalming, and desire to avoid heavy expense, the embalmers

---

* Asiri.

proceed in the following manner; by means of syringes they inject cedar oil into the abdomen of the dead without opening it or removing the entrails, and they take care to retain the liquid in such manner that none of it may escape. They next plunge the body into carbonate of soda and leave it there for the time specified, and then cause the cedar oil which they first introduced, to issue from its cavities. The latter has strength enough to carry with it the intestines and the viscera, for it liquefies them all. Externally, the soda has dried up the flesh, and nothing remains of the dead man but his skin and his bones : these operations concluded, they deliver the body and their task is over.

LXXXVIII. The third style of embalming, for the accommodation of the poor, is this : the embalmers make an injection of horse-radish into the intestines, and dry the body in carbonate of soda for seventy days ; then they deliver it.

XC. Whoever is found dead after having been seized by a crocodile, or swept away by the river, be he Egyptian or stranger, and whatever the town where his body was picked up, is entitled to consecrated burial at the hands of the inhabitants. They perform the funeral rites in the costliest manner and deposit the body in their burial chambers. Neither its friends nor its neighbors are permitted to touch it, but the priests of the Nile take charge of it and bury it as a more than human body.—*Herodotus, Book II.*

The foregoing facts were gleaned by the historian of Halicarnassus in the midst of Egyptian society when it had grown old and was in full decay : they may be completed by other information deduced from the paintings on the walls so abundant on the monuments which that same social organization reared in the days of its youth and development. In this respect, what is there more curious or more striking from the point of view afforded by the private and civic life of the primitive Egyptians than the sepulchral grottoes of

Beni Hassan, excavated on the right bank of the Nile, not far from the ancient Artemidos? Below we give, according to Champollion, an enumeration of the subjects represented on the walls of these hypogees.

I. *Agriculture.*—Designs representing ploughing done by oxen or by human labor; sowing, the treading of the ground by rams, and not by pigs as Herodotus says; five kinds of carts; digging and the harvest of grain and flax; the sheaving of these different kinds of plants; the stacking, the threshing and pounding, the measuring and the housing of the same in barns; two designs of different kinds of large barns; flax carried by asses; a host of other agricultural toils, and among them the gathering of the lotus; the cultivation of the vine, the vintage, its transportation, the seeding, the winepress of two kinds, one by manual power, the other by machinery; the bottling of the wine, or putting up in jars, and its conveyance to the cellar; the manufacture of shrub, etc., garden culture, the gathering of fruit, the cultivation of the onion, irrigation, etc.; all, like the following pictures, with explanatory hieroglyphic legends; and, moreover, the superintendent of the country house and his clerks.

II. *Trades and Manufactures.*—A collection of paintings, mostly in colors, so as to the better determine the nature of the articles, and representing the carver in stone and the carver in wood, the painter of statues, the painter of architectural objects; furniture and cabinet work, the painter with his pallet executing a picture; scribes and clerks busied with writings of all kinds; workmen at the quarries carrying blocks of stone; the potter's trade with all its operations; workmen kneading clay with their feet, others with their hands; the placing of the clay on the conical wheel and the wheel on the turning lathe, the potter making the belly and the neck of the vase, etc.: the first baking in the kiln, the second drying in the oven; makers of canes, oars and paddles; cabinet makers; joiners; carpenters; wood-sawyers; curriers; the leather and morocco dyers; the shoemaker; spinning; the weaving of cloths of different manufacture;

the glassblower and all his operations; the goldsmith, the jeweller; the blacksmith.

III. *The Military Caste.*—The education of the military caste and all its gymnastic exercises, represented in more than 200 pictures, in which are reproduced all the positions and attitudes that two skillful antagonists can assume, attacking, defending, receding, advancing, standing up, prostrate etc.; people may see from these whether Egyptian art contented itself with mere profile designs, legs joined and arms tightly pressed against the haunches.

I copied all this curious series of naked warriors struggling together; and, besides, some sixty figures representing soldiers of every arm and of every rank; sham fights; a siege; the tortoise and the battering ram; military punishments; a field of battle and the preparations for a military meal; finally, the manufacture of spears, javelins, bows, arrows, war clubs, battle-axes, etc.

IV. *Singing, Music and Dancing.*—A picture representing a vocal and instrumental concert; a singer whom a musician accompanies on the harp, is seconded by two choirs, one of four men, the other of five women, and the latter beat the time of the measure with their hands: it is a whole opera; harp players of both sexes; players of the German flute, of the flageolet, of a species of conch shell, etc.; dancers executing different figures with the names of the steps they are dancing; in fine, a very curious collection of designs representing dancing women (or *almés* of ancient Egypt) dancing, singing, playing tennis and performing divers feats of strength and skill.

V. A considerable number of designs representing the *education of animals;* cowherds with oxen of all kinds, cows, calves; milking; butter and cheese making; goatherds; keepers of asses; shepherds and their sheep; scenes relating to the veterinary art; finally, the barn yard, comprising the management of a great variety of geese and ducks, and of a species of swan that had been domesticated in ancient Egypt.

VII. Designs relative to *games, exercises, and amusements.* Among these may be noticed a sort of "hot cockles," "sledge-hammer," jackstraws, the game of pegs driven into the ground, etc.; different games of strength; the chase of wild beasts, a picture representing a grand hunt on the desert, and in which from 15 to 20 kinds of quadrupeds are depicted; scenes representing the return from the chase; the game carried in dead or brought alive; many pictures representing the pursuit of birds with the net; one of these paintings is of very large dimensions and is filled out with all the colors, and the movement of the original. Finally, drawings on a large scale, of the different kinds of traps to take birds, are given: these instruments of the chase are painted, separately, in some hypogees. Then, there are many pictures that relate to fishing; line angling; the line and fishing rod; fishing with the trident or bident; with the net; the preparation of fish, etc.

VIII. *Domestic Justice.*—Under this head, I have arranged some fifteen designs of bas-reliefs representing offences committed by servants; the arrest of the culprit: the charge against him; his defence; his conviction by the superintendents of the household; his condemnation and punishment, which is restricted to the bastinado, the minutes of which, along with all the particulars, have to be deposited with the body of the trial in the hands of the master of the house by his superintendent.

IX. *The House and Housekeeping.*—I have brought together in this series, which is very numerous already, everything that relates to private or interior home life. These very curious designs represent, 1st, different Egyptian houses, more or less sumptuous; 2nd, vases of different forms, utensils and furniture, all colored, because the colors invariably indicate the material; 3d, a splendid palanquin; 4th, a kind of small room with folding doors borne along on a sledge and serving as vehicles for the great personages of Egypt in ancient times; 5th, monkeys, cats and dogs which formed part of the household, as well as dwarfs and other human deformities who served to clear the spleen of the Egyptian lords 1500 years B. C. just as they did for the old style barons in Europe 1500 years after the birth of the Saviour ; 6th, the officers of a great establishment, superintendents, clerks, etc.; 7th, servants carrying in supplies of all kinds for the table ; the maids likewise bringing various eatables ; 8th, the mode of slaughtering beef and cutting it up for home use ; 9th, a series of designs representing cooks preparing dishes of different kinds ; 10th and last, servants bringing the dishes all prepared to the master's table.

XII. *Navigation.*—An assortment of designs representing the construction of vessels and barks of different kinds, and the games of the sailors, altogether analogous to the contests of strength and skill that take place on the Seine on great holidays.—*Champollion's Letters from Egypt and Nubia.*

In a crypt of the strange necropolis that has furnished these details, the mortal remains of a governor of the *nome* of *Sah* had been *sealed up* for *all eternity.* The deceased informs us, by the history of his life written on the walls of *his eternal abode*, what were the duties and conduct of an important functionary of the military caste, at that remote period.

. . . As a general, he had accompanied the king (an Usertesen of the 15th dynasty) into the land of Cush, and had penetrated *to the extremities of the earth.* Subsequently, at the head of a troop of 400 men, he had brought back from the mines on the Peninsula of Sinai a convoy of gold to the city of Keft (Coptos.) As *nomarch* (or governor of a *nome*) he had earned the praises of his sovereign and the gratitude of his constituency.

"I," he says, " was a master full of goodness and amiability; a governor who loved his country. For years I exercised my power in the nome of *Sah.* All the works for the royal house were executed through my care. Thanks were extended to me on the part of the royal house for the tribute brought in by me in horned cattle. I carried the fr*y* of all my toil to the royal house. Nothing was stolen from me in all my workshops. I labored and the whole nome was in activity. Never was a little child distressed by me; never was a widow maltreated by me; never have I troubled a fisherman on the waters or a shepherd in the pasture fields. Never was there a pentarch (foreman of five) whose men I turned aside from their work. Never was there a scarcity in my time, never a starving mouth under my administration, even if these were famine years. For, see, I had tilled all the fields of the nome of *Sah* clear to its frontiers on the north and on the south. I made its inhabitants live upon its products, and thus there were no starving people in it. I gave equally to the widow and to the married woman, nor did I set the great before the little in the distributions that I made. And, see, the Nile was in great inundation; the owners of the fields and of the orchards were full of hope for a fertile year, and I did not cut the branches of the canal. etc. etc."

The last part of this curious inscription in which the nomarch, referring to a famine that took place during the years of his administration, makes a panegyric in his own behalf, for having warded off the miseries of the dearth by his benevolent impartiality toward every one, has struck some observers as a pendant to the history of Joseph in Egypt and his seven famous years of famine in that country.

A mural scene on the same tomb recalls still more vividly the Biblical legend. It represents the arrival in Egypt of a family of the Semitic race of the *Aam* or Ammonites. Forced by causes unknown, by a famine, perhaps, they have, like the sons of Jacob, abandoned their country; they present themselves, thirty-seven persons in number—men, women and children—before Chnumhotep, the governor of the nome of *Sah*, to solicit help or an asylum at his hands. A temple scribe called *Neferhotep* is offering to the nomarch a sheet of papyrus covered with an inscription bearing at

Nomads from Asia coming into Egypt to solicit an asylum from the governor of a province.

the top the date of the year six of *Usertesen* II., and the number of the strangers. The chief or *sheik* of the little tribe, named *Abu-sa*, first respectfully approaches the person of *Chnumhotep* and offers him a young wild-goat as a present. Behind him are his companions armed with spears, clubs and bows; their women clad in richly colored tunics, and their children carried in wicker paniers slung over the backs of donkeys. The musician and minstrel of the clan closes the march playing on a sort of lyre.

Are not these the pioneers, or, if the term be preferable, the forlorn hope of the vanguard of those nomadic hordes which were, at a later period, to inundate the valley of the Nile?

X.

THE details collected by Herodotus with regard to the civil and private life of the Egyptians are of nine centuries later date than the epoch of Rameses Mei-Amoun. Those which the grottoes of Beni-Hassan yield us relate to generations long preceding that conqueror. Nevertheless, the lapse of time does not appear to have introduced any noticeable dissimilarities between them. We think that we can fill them out with ideas upon the connection of temples with temples and the diplomatic relations of sovereigns with sovereigns at a period of history when the sceptre of Egypt was still held by the Pharaohs of the name and blood of Rameses.

These items of information are yielded us by a *stele* found at Thebes among the ruins of a temple of *Khons*, a divinity who appears to have been the object of a special kind of worship, and to have enjoyed a renown that was propagated as far as the centre of Asia.

THE STELE OF THE TEMPLE OF KHONS.

. . . . His Majesty Rameses XII. having gone to *Naharina* (Mesopotamia) to collect the annual tribute of that region, the princes and chiefs of each province came to prostrate themselves before him, and the natives of inferior rank, stooping beneath burthens of gold, of lapis lazuli, of copper and of precious woods, drew near to lay them at his feet.

The King of Bouchten (Ecbatana according to Dr. Brugsch) came, in his turn, to do homage to His Majesty and to solicit peace. He had with him his eldest daughter, a young and handsome woman, who at once captivated the heart of Rameses more than did anything else. His Majesty gave her the title of *Great Queen*, the name of Ra-Neferu, and conducted her to Egypt, where she was received with solemn pomp.

In the fifteenth year of his reign, when His Majesty was celebrating at Thebes—that capital and mistress of the nations—the grand panegyric of his father Ammon, the sun, the distributor of thrones, behold the arrival of a messenger bearing rich presents from the King of Bouchten for the queen, was announced to his Majesty.

On being admitted to the presence of Rameses XII., the envoy saluted His Majesty in these words: "Glory to thee, oh sun of nine peoples; grant to us the breath of life!" Then prostrating himself, he added: "The king my master sends me to Thy Holiness because of Benten-rest, the young sister of the Queen Ra-Neferu. A secret malady consumes her; will Thy Holiness deign to send to her one of those men who know all things, such as there are around thee?"

Then the King said: "Let there be assembled before me the college of sacred philosophers and the doctors skilled in mysteries."

So soon as they had all hastened to stand in array in His Majesty's presence, he said to them: "I have summoned you to hear and to obey. Point out to me the one of all of you whom you look upon as the firmest of heart, the quickest in understanding and the most skillful of hand."

The recorder of sacred writings, Toth-em-hebi, stepped forth from the ranks and bowed before His Majesty. He immediately received orders to repair to the country of Bouchten with the royal messenger.

But when this master of wisdom and science had arrived at Bouchten, and was placed in the presence of the spirit that beset the Princess Benten-rest, he found himself its inferior and dared not engage in contest with it.

The King of Bouchten thereupon sent another messenger to Pharaoh, saying : "Sovereign lord ! oh my master ! deign to command that a god may be brought to the country of Bouchten to combat this evil spirit."

His Holiness was then still at Thebes, celebrating, in the twenty-sixth year of his reign, the panegyric of Ammon. He thereupon went to the temple of the Theban god Khons-Neferhotep, and thus appealed to him : " O my beneficent Lord ! I come to thee on behalf of the daughter of the King of Bouchten. If thou wouldst command Khonsou, the giver of counsel who subdues rebels, to go to the country of Bouchten, endowng him with some of thy divine power, I will cause that god to be borne thither to save the daughter of the king my father-in-law."

Khons-Neferhotep, the patron of Thebes, acquiesced in His Majesty's wishes, and, four times over, imparted a portion of his divine virtue to the god Khonsou-Pa-ar-secher, who, enclosed in a brilliant *naos*, and placed upon a grand *bari*, proceeded upon a broad car toward the country of Bouchten, escorted by many horsemen riding on the right and on the left of him.

When, at the end of a year and five months, the god Khonsou-Pa-ar-secher arrived in the country of Bouchten, the king, accompanied by his chieftains and his soldiers, came forth to meet him, and, prostrating himself before the sacred *bari*, cried aloud with his forehead in the dust : "Hail to thee, who comest to us by order of the King Rameses !"

When the god had reached the place where the Princess Benten-rest was, the spirit that beset her humiliated itself before Khonsou-Pa-ar-secher, and said to him : " Welcome to thee, mighty god, conqueror of those who rebel ! The **strong** city of Bouchten is thy domain ; its inhabitants bow down before thee, and for myself, I am thy slave ; I shall be no hindrance to the purpose of thy journey, but shall return to the place whence I came. Only command the King of Bouchten to make a sacrifice in my honor."

Then Khonsou-Pa-ar-secher of Thebes said graciously to his prophet : "Let the King of Bouchten make a sacrifice honorable to this spirit."

While the god Khonsou and the spirit were thus conversing, the King of Bouchten, filled with a holy fear, was trembling in the midst of his soldiers. He celebrated a great festival in honor of Khonsou and of the spirit, made rich offerings to them, and his daughter Benten-rest was instantly cured, and the spirit withdrew whither he saw fit.

Then the King of Bouchten was seized with extreme delight, as also were all his subjects. Then he said : "This god ought to remain in the country of Bouchten. I will not let him go back to Egypt." Thus Khonsou-Pa-ar-secher was kept three years and nine months in Bouchten ; but at the end of that time, behold the King of Bouchten, lying in his bed, saw this god leaving his *naos* in the form of a golden sparrow-hawk, and extending his wings to fly toward Egypt. And the king, when he awoke, was seized with an inward sickness. He then said to the priest of Khonsou-Pa-ar-secher : "Let him leave us quickly and return to Egypt : cause his car to be made ready !"

When the King of Bouchten caused this god to depart for Egypt, he gave him numerous and costly presents, and soldiers and horses in great quantity. And when the god Khonsou-Pa-ar-secher had reached the temple of Khons-Neferhotep, he offered him the presents which the King of Bouchten had given him in the form of all sorts of good things, and kept nothing for himself. Khonsou-Pa-ar-secher of Thebes thus returned to his temple in peace in the year 33, on the nineteenth day of the month of Mechir, of the King Rameses XII., reigning eternally like the sun.

CHRONOLOGICAL CANON,

OR

TABLE OF THE DYNASTIES AND KINGS OF EGYPT

FROM MENES DOWN TO CAMBYSES, ACCORDING TO MANETHO AND JULIUS THE AFRICAN.

NAMES IN MANETHO.	MONUMENTAL NAMES.	Years assigned.	SYNCHRONISMS AND OBSERVATIONS.
1st Dynasty.—Thinite.			
Menes.	Mena. A.-Taund.	253	Menes, the successor in Egypt of Asiri the son and god of the dead, belongs to the first Vedic tradition, like the Sanscrit Manu, son of the Sun and brother of the Asura Yama, the god of the dead; like the Manes of Lydia, son of Chronos; like the Cretan Menes, son of Zeus; the Minyas of Iolcus, son of a Titan, and the Manus of Germany, son of Chaos. The name of Athot or AT-aud signifies, according to Eratosthenes, the learned librarian of Alexandria, descendant or son of Mercury.
Athotis.			
Kenchenes.			
Ouenephes.			
Ousaphaes.			
Miebis.			
Semempses.			
Bieneches.			

NAMES IN MANETHO.	MONUMENTAL NAMES.	Years assigned.	SYNCHRONISMS AND OBSERVATIONS.
2d Dynasty.—Thinite.			
Boethos.	Bau.		Is it by the effect of chance simply that three names of this dynasty, contain the radical *kai* or *ke*, which signifies *large* or *giant* in Pehlvi an l in old Armenian? Is it not rather a mark of origin? Did not the same flood of Turanian emigration which deposited the *Kauans* in Bactria and in Media, carry some of them to the banks of the Nile with their primitive god—fire?
Kaiechos.	.... [kai-i-kal]		
Binothris.			
Tlas.			
Sethenes.	Send. .... kai-ra.	302	
Chaires.			
Nephercheres.	.... kai-ra.		
Sesochris.			
Cheneres.	.... kai-n-ra.		
3d Dynasty.—Memphite.			
Necherop.			
Tosorthros.		214	
Tyris.			
Mesochris.			
Syphis.			
Tosertasis.			
Aches.			
Sephouris.	Snefrou ?.........		*This king, the first of whom epigraphy has has found certain traces, seems to have reigned over Lower Egypt and the peninsula of Sinai. He should be transferred to the head of the IV Dynasty. The first double use ascertained in the lists.
Kerpheres.*			
4th Dynasty.—Memphite.		294	
Soris.	Snefru.		1st. The three first reigns of this dynasty present a total of 158 years. How much must be deducted from this cipher to make it agree with an inscription on a tomb of Gizeh, which shows the Queen *Meri-tefs* living in these three successive reigns?
Souphis I., or (Cheops).	Chufiu, Chnum-Chufru.	29	
Souphis II.	Chafra. (Chpe-hren).	63	2d. According to Manetho, Herodotus and Diodorus, the three kings who constructed the great Pyramids, form but two generations,
Mencheres.	Men-ka-ra.	66	
		63	

NAMES IN MANETHO.	MONUMENTAL NAMES.	Years assigned.	SYNCHRONISMS AND OBSERVATIONS.
4th Dynasty.—Memphite.			
Ratoises.	Ratuf.		Chafra being the brother, and Men-ka-ra, the son of Chufu [for Cheops]; how much must be deducted to render acceptable to serious history the total of 192 years assigned to them in the opposite column?
Bicheres.	} Azeskaf.		
Sebercheres.			
Thamphthis.			
5th Dynasty.—Elephantine.			
Ouserchers.	User-kaf.		Manetho causes the mention of this dynasty and of the following one of Elephantina, and ascribes to them the Southern extremity of Egypt as the centre of their power. Mr. Brugsch carries both of them to Memphis because the kings that compose them have their burial place in that city. This is a question of principle very open to discussion. At that first epoch of the regulation of Egyptian society, when all the living fetiches of the Egyptian clans—cats, dogs, jackals, ibis, ichneumons, oxen, crocodiles, had their places of burial marked in a certain appointed spot in the valley of the Nile, why should not the kings, princes, and petty rulers of that same valley, wish to be interred together in one place, consecrated for religious or traditional motives?
Sephres.	S hu-ra.		
Nephercheres.	Nefer ur-ka-ra.	198	
Sisires.	Alites.		
Cheres.	0 0 0		
Rathonres.	Kannu-r.		
Mencheres.	Menkahor.		
Tatcheres.	Tatkrara.		
Onnos.	Unas.		
6th Dynasty.—Memphite.			
Othoes.	Teta.	203	This dynasty is one of the two most curious to study. 1st, It opens with a king killed by his guards on account of his tyranny. 2d, it contains two names: Mentu-hotep belonging to the 11th dynasty, the contemporaneousness of which is proved by by this fact. 3d, A *stele* relating to a great dignitary named Una, who lived under the kings, Teta, Papi and Ramcri, proves superabundantly that these kings succeeded each other without discontinuation, and how much faith is to be placed in the 100 years of the reign of the second of them. We should not speak of Queen Nitocris, if Herodotus had not mentioned her as coming from Babylon, which would indicate an intrusion of Asiatics into Egypt about that period.
Phios.	Mentuhotep.	36	
Methosouphis.	Pepi.	53	
Phiops.	Rameri.	100	
Menthesouphis.	Nit-aker.	"	
Nitocris.	Nefer-ka.	12	
	Nefcres.		

290   APPENDIX.

NAMES IN MANETHO.	MONUMENTAL NAMES.	Years assigned.	SYNCHRONISMS AND OBSERVATIONS.
7th Dynasty.—Memphite. 70 kings in 70 days!!! 9 kings.			
8th Dynasty.—Memphite. 4 kings.	Unknown.	146	These and the following (8th to 10th) dynasties reigned side by side in different provinces of Egypt. Epigraphy readily makes this concession to history.
9th Dynasty.—Heracleopolite, or of Fayoum. 4 kings.		100	
10th Dynasty.—Heracleopolite. 19 kings.	Unknown.	185	
11th Dynasty.—Theban. 6 kings.	According to the canon at Turin.	43	According to the monuments, it is in this dynasty that we must range the Mentou-Hotep put by Manetho in the 6th.

NAMES IN MANETHO.	MONUMENTAL NAMES.	Years assigned.	SYNCHRONISMS AND OBSERVATIONS.
12th Dynasty.—Theban.			
1. [Ammenemes.]	Amenemha I.	213	This dynasty is placed at Thebes, but most of the monuments that it has left are met with in the Fayoum.
2. Sesonchis,	Usertesen I.		
3. Ammanemes.	Amenemha II.		
4. Sesostris,	Usertesen II.		
5. Lamares,	Usertesen III.		
6. Ameres,	Amenemha III.		
7. Amenemes.	Amenemha IV.		
8. Skemiophris.	Ra-sebek-nefru.		
13th Dynasty.—Theban.			
60 kings.	Among them: Sebek-hotep I.	353	The territorial unity attempted by the XII. dynasty falls under the following dynasties, and a feudal anarchy prevails in Upper and Lower Egypt, the invasion and conquest of which by the nomads of the East it facilitates.
	Sebek-hotep II.		
	Sebek-hotep III.		
	Sebek-hotep IV.		
	Sebek-hotep V. Nefer-hotep I.		
	Sebek-hotep VI. Sebek-hotep VII.		
	Sebek-hotep VIII.		

APPENDIX.

NAMES IN MANETHO.	MONUMENTAL NAMES.	Years assigned.	SYNCHRONISMS AND OBSERVATIONS.
14th Dynasty.—Xoite. 76 kings in Lower Egypt.		484	A dynasty contemporaneous with the preceding one and with the invasion of the Hycsos.
15th Dynasty; } **Theban.** **16th Dynasty;** }		260	These two dynasties, driven out of Egypt by an Asiatic invasion, lived parallel to the following, composed of foreign conquerors.
17th Dynasty.—Hycsos. 1. Salatis. 2. Beon. 3. Apachnas. 4. Apophis. 5. Jannas. 6. Assis.	Apapias. Asseth?	242	The conqueror of the Hycsos and who drove them out. His widow regent under the following reign. Thothmes I. reigned conjointly with his sister Ahmense-Hatasou, regent under Thothmes II., and until the 22d year of Thotimes III. For the time elapsing between Aahmes and Thothmes III., we have a precious document in the biographical stele of Aahmes, chief of the marine, who
18th Dynasty.—Theban. Amosis. Chebron. Amenophis.	Aahmes. Nefru-ari. Amenoph I.		

APPENDIX.

18th Dynasty.—(*Continued.*)

NAMES IN MANETHO.	MONUMENTAL NAMES.	Years assigned.	SYNCHRONISMS AND OBSERVATIONS.
Amesses.	Thothmes I.		born under Prince Rasekenen, the prince or *ha* of Upper Egypt, before the expulsion of the Hycsos, lived and served successively under the four first kings of the XVIIIth dynasty. Amenoph III. is the Memnon of the Greeks. The reforms that he wished to introduce into the worship arouse a revolt and four usurping kings reign over Egypt at the same time as Horemheb. The XVIIIth dynasty ends amid civil and religious troubles.
Mephres.	Thothmes II.		
Mephramouthosis.	Thothmes III.	242	
Thmosis.	Amenoph II.		
Amenophi.	Thothmes IV.		
Horus.	Amenoph III.		
Akencheres.	Horemheb.		
Rathothis.	Usurping kings, contemporaries of Horemheb.		
Akenchercs.			
Akencheres.			

Note. Upon the island of Elephantine, king Thothmes III. had caused a temple to be erected to the god of the cataracts, Chnum, but only a few detached stones now remain of it. On one of these there is clearly to be read the following inscription: "On the 29th day of the month Epiphi, the day of the appearance of the star Sopd (Sothis :) festival." The illustrious French astronomer, Biot, whom the whole historical importance of this date could not escape, subjected it to astronomical calculation. According to him this rising of Sirius must have taken place in the year 1444, before the Christian Era. This date admitted, the whole chronology of the XVIIIth dynasty would be in full disagreement with the astronomical result. But we should remark that according to the observations of Lepsius, who has fixed the epoch of Tothmosis from 1603 to 1565, the Egyptian sculptor employed to carve the date in question upon the above-mentioned stone, committed a serious error, by adding a third small line which would go to indicate the third instead of the second month of the tetrarchy of heat. This would change the month Epiphi to Paoni, and the date 1444 to that of 1580 or 1574 B. C. This supposition is, no doubt, very ingenious; but its only basis is a very slender line! However, we do not see how, without the hypothesis of the learned Prussian, we could manage to logically array in line, in less than a century and a half, all the names and all the facts comprised in the lapse of time between Thothmes III. and the XXth dynasty, which commences with the year 1300.

294 APPENDIX.

NAMES IN MANETHO.	MONUMENTAL NAMES.	Years assigned.	SYNCHRONISMS AND OBSERVATIONS.
19th Dynasty.—Theban.			
Ramesea.	Ramessu I.		Legitimate inheritor of the XVIIIth dynasty.
Sethos.	Seti I.		
Rampses.	Ramessu II.	170	*Rameses, Mei-Amoun* or *Sesostris* (1400—1339 B. C.)
Menephthes.	Merneptah I.		
[Sethos.]	Seti II.		Civil and religious troubles.
Amenemes.	{ Merneptah II.		
	Amenemses.		Epoch of Moses; the descendants of Rameses are obliged to take
Thouoris.	Siptah and his wife.		refuge in Nubia for 13 years.
	Tauser.		
20th Dynasty.—Diospolite.			
	1. Rameses III.		The date of the year 1300 B. C., calculated by Biot, falls in the reign of
	2. Rameses IV.		this king. (The first certain date of Egyptian history.
	3. Rameses V.		
	4. Rameses VI.		
	5. Rameses VII.	178	The year 1240 B. C., the 2d certain date calculated by Biot, belongs to
	6. Rameses VIII.		this reign.
	7. Tum-Merji.		
	8. Rameses IX.		
	9. Rameses X.		With this dynasty ends the supremacy of Egypt over Mesopotamia—
	10. Rameses XI.		probable epoch of the foundation of Nineveh and of the reign of
	11. Rameses XII.		Ninus of classical fame. (1200–1150 B. C.)
	12. Rameses XIII.		

APPENDIX.

NAMES IN MANETHO.	MONUMENTAL NAMES.	Years assigned.	SYNCHRONISMS AND OBSERVATIONS.
21st Dynasty.—Tanite.			
Smendes.	Ba-n-ded (?)	130	Rival Dynasty of the high priests of Thebes.
Psousennes.	(Nefer-ka-ra.)		
Nephercheres.	(Meri-n-ptah.		Pe-hor.
Amenophthis.	Uasorkun.		Pai-banch.
Osorcho.	P-seb-n-cha.		Pai-n-Tchen.
Psinaches.	Sasanq, regent.		Ba-men-chepar.
Psousennes.			
22d Dynasty.—Bubastite.			
Sesonchoris.	Sasanq I.	120	Takes Jerusalem, and holds king Rehoboam for a ransom about 974 B.C. It is common consent to identify Ua-sork-an with Serak, who, according to the Chronicles of Kings, ch. xiv., was defeated near Maresa, by Asa, king of Judah, about the year 950 B.C.
Osorthon.	Uasorkun.		
	Takelot I.		
Anonymous kings.	Uasorkun.		
Takelothis.	Sasanq II.		Under this and the following dynasty, the decadence of Egypt went on with accelerated speed, the vassal peoples shook off the yoke, and a rival power arose in Ethiopia.
	Takelot II.		
	Sasanq III.		
Anonymous kings.	Pachj.		
	Sasanq IV.		
23d Dynasty.—Tanite.			
Petonbaetes.	Petsabast.	89	While the Egyptians lacked a fixed era to which they could assign the dates of each reign, the Greeks contemporaneous with Petsabast founded the era of the Olympiads. (776 B.C.)
Osorchon.	Uasorkan.		Era of the foundation of Rome 754.
Psammus.	Psamut.		The Chaldean era of Nabonatzar 747.
Zet [Thephachthus.]			

NAMES IN MANETHO.	MONUMENTAL NAMES.	Years assigned.	SYNCHRONISMS AND OBSERVATIONS.
24th Dynasty.—Saitic.			
Bocchoris.	Bek-n-renf.	6	Is dethroned and burnt alive by the Ethiopians.
25th Dynasty.—Ethiopian.			
Sabakon.	Sabaka.	50	Egypt is conquered by the Ethiopians about the year 715 B. C. Hosea, king of Israel, asks the aid of Seva the Cushite (Sabataga) against the Assyrian Salmanatzar, about the year 700. Tahaiqa, about the year 690, repulses an attack of Sennacherib.
Sevikos.	Sabataga.		
Tarkos.	Tahaiqa.		
26th Dynasty.—Saitic.			
Stephinates.	Planch1?	138	Psammetik I. repels an invasion of the Scythians toward 625. Nekau II., marching against Nineveh, is attacked by Josias, King of Jerusalem : he defeats and kills him at Megiddo in 610. He is himself defeated by Nebuchadnezzar at Karkemish (Circessium) about the year 606 B. C.
Nechopsos.			
Nechao I.	Nekau I.		
Psammeticus I.	Psemtek I.		
Nechao II.	Nekau II.		
Psammeticus II.	Psemtek II.		
Ouapris.	Uahhepra.		
Amosis.	Aahme.		
Psammecherites.	Psemtek III.		

Conquest of Egypt by Cambyses in the year 527 B. C., and the end of Ancient Egypt.

A NEW AND REVISED ISSUE OF

THE ILLUSTRATED LIBRARY OF WONDERS.

THE WONDERS OF MAN AND NATURE,
IN EIGHT VOLUMES.

THE WONDERS OF SCIENCE,
IN EIGHT VOLUMES.

THE WONDERS OF ART AND ARCHÆOLOGY,
IN EIGHT VOLUMES.

Twenty-four volumes, containing over a Thousand Valuable Illustrations.

EACH VOLUME 12mo, COMPLETE IN ITSELF.

Sold Separately at $1.00 per Volume.

Messrs. CHARLES SCRIBNER'S SONS have now begun the publishing of a new and revised edition of a series of books the success of which has been most extraordinary and lasting. THE WONDER LIBRARY brings within popular comprehension the various operations and procedures in Science and the Arts, the phenomena and laws of nature, curious and striking facts

ILLUSTRATED LIBRARY OF WONDERS.

in natural history, remarkable exploits, archæological discoveries, and a historical account of the progress of the fine arts.

The volumes are written by a number of French scientists and specialists of the highest rank, and translated and adapted for English readers by competent hands.

The subjects treated are of universal interest, and they are discussed in the popular and entertaining manner in which the French excel, and which is peculiarly adapted to interest the young, and develop their taste for studies of this character, as well as to instruct older readers.

The illustrations are so numerous that they present every phase of science with accuracy and completeness; they add materially to the attractiveness and value of the series, which is by far the most thorough, interesting and valuable of the kind ever produced.

The new edition, published at a low price, has been prepared to supply the continuous and large demand which has always existed for these books.

The great advance which of late years has been made in the Natural Sciences has offered the opportunity to greatly enrich several of the volumes, by presenting to the reader the result of the latest researches, written by experienced pens. The numerous additions have made the volumes more valuable than they ever were before; and in the cheap but substantial form in which they are now issued, they are sure of a new and increased popularity.

Illustrated Library of Wonders.

THE WONDERS OF MAN AND NATURE.

Wonders of the Human Body.
Bodily Strength and Skill.
The Sublime in Nature.
Mountain Adventures.
Adventures on the Great Hunting Grounds.
Wonderful Escapes.
The Intelligence of Animals.
Thunder and Lightning.

THE WONDERS OF SCIENCE.

Wonders of Electricity.
Wonders of Heat.
The Sun.
Wonders of the Moon.
Wonders of Optics.
Wonders of Acoustics.
Wonders of the Heavens.
Wonders of Water.

THE WONDERS OF ART AND ARCHÆOLOGY.

Wonders of European Art.
Wonders of Italian Art.
Wonders of Architecture.
Wonders of Sculpture.
Wonders of Engraving.
Wonders of Glass Making.
Pompeii and the Pompeians.
Egypt 3300 Years Ago.

Illustrated Library of Wonders.

To be published in SEPTEMBER:

Intelligence of Animals, with Illustrative Anecdotes. From the French of ERNEST MENAUT. With 54 Illustrations. 12mo.

Wonders of Heat. By ACHILLE CAZIN. With 93 Illustrations, and colored frontispiece. 12mo.

Egypt 3,300 Years Ago; or, Rameses the Great. By F. DELANOYE. With 40 illustrations. 12mo.

To be published in OCTOBER:

Mountain Adventures. Compiled from the Note-Books of Distinguished Travelers, including Whymper and Tyndall. Edited with additions by Hon. J. T. HEADLEY. With 41 illustrations. 12mo.

Wonders of the Heavens. By CAMILLE FLAMMARION. Translated from the French by Mrs. NORMAN LOCKYER. With 48 illustrations. 12mo.

The Wonders of Sculpture. From the French of LOUIS VIARDOT. With a Chapter on American Sculpture. With 62 illustrations. 12mo.

A volume in each of the three series will be issued monthly, until the entire library is completed in this new edition.

PRICE, PER VOLUME, $1.00.

** *For sale by all booksellers, or will be sent, post-paid, on receipt of price, by*

CHARLES SCRIBNER'S SONS,

743-745 Broadway, New York.

www.ingramcontent.com/pod-product-compliance
Lightning Source LLC
Chambersburg PA
CBHW030820230426
43667CB00008B/1304